ENGLISH LINGUISTICS
1500—1800

(A Collection of Facsimile Reprints)

Selected and Edited by

R. C. ALSTON

No. 325

THE SCOLAR PRESS LIMITED
MENSTON, ENGLAND
1972

NIELS HEMMINGSEN

THE PREACHER

1574

A Scolar Press Facsimile

THE SCOLAR PRESS LIMITED
MENSTON, ENGLAND
1972

THE SCOLAR PRESS LIMITED
20 Main Street, Menston, Yorkshire, England

SBN 85417 686 1

Printed in Great Britain by
The Scolar Press Limited
Menston, Yorkshire, England

NOTE

Reproduced (original size) by permission of the Syndics of Cambridge University Library. Shelf-mark: Syn. 8.57.117.

Niels Hemmingsen (Hemmingius) was one of the few sixteenth century rhetorical theorists to produce a treatise on pulpit eloquence. This work was first published as part of Hemmingsen's important *De methodis libri duo* published at Leipzig in 1565 (there is a copy in the library of Trinity College, Cambridge), and reprinted there in 1578. Many of his treatises were translated into English and John Horsfall's translation of *Ecclesiasten*, the original title, was one of the earliest.

Unlike many treatments of pulpit oratory Hemmingsen's is systematic and stands in the Ciceronian tradition and in this sense can be seen as an important source for William Perkins' *Prophetica* (1592) later translated into English by Thomas Tuke as *The Arte of Prophecying* (1606).

The *Preacher* is a rare work (four copies of the first edition, and two of the second (1576) are recorded), and has never been reprinted.

References: STC 13265; Alston, VI, 265.

THE PREA-cher, or Methode of preaching,

vvrytten in Latine by Nicholas Hemminge, and tranſlated into Engliſhe by I. H. Very neceſſarie for al thoſe that by the true preaching of the word of God, labour to pull downe the Sinagoge of Sathan, and to buylde vp the Temple of GOD.

I. Corinth. I. 18.

The preaching of the Croſſe, is to thé that periſhe fooliſhneſſe: but vnto vs vvhich are ſaued, it is the povver of God.

Seene and alowed according to the Queenes Maieſties Iniunction.

¶ *Imprinted at London by*
Thomas Marſhe.
Anno. 1574.
Cum Priuilegio.

To the right Honourable Dougles Lady Sheffeld, late wyfe of Lord Iohn Sheffeld disceased: Iohn Horsfall, her most humble and faithfull seruaunt wisheth all health and godlines long to continue vvith increase of vertue and zeale in Religion.

(*.*.*)

After that I had by the good aduise and earnest persuation of certaine of my brethren Ministers of this citty of London trãslated out of latine into our vulgar tongue this litle booke intituled The preacher or Methode of preaching &c. necessary for all those ẏ by the true & sincere preaching of the worde, labour to pull downe the sinagogue of Satan and to build vp the temple of God, I thought

 it my

it my bounden duty (right Honourable and my singuler good Lady) to dedicate ỹ same vnto your honour, and that for diuers and sondrye causes. VVher of the first and chiefest is that zeale and godlines in the true religiō & fayth of our sauiour Christ, which I by experience haue noted and foūd to be such in you, that you do not onely your selfe dailye serue God by prayer, but do also straightly commaunde all your family and see them do the same. Imitating herein the example of the faythfull father of all the Sonnes of God Abrahā, who did not onely himselfe but also appointed his whole family which was greate to serue God daily. The second cause is ỹ correctiō of sinne, by displacinge and puttinge cleane out of your house al such which by their vngodlines might either brīg vppon themselues the iuste plague of Almighty God, or els be an euill exā-ple vnto others to cōmit the like. The third is your honours gret meekenes, patience and modestye towardes all mē and in all your affayres. The last cause is for ẏ it pleased your honour of your goodnes & mere liberality to accepte and take me to be your house-hold Chaplaine, & as it were a guide and helper of that godly zeale of cal-ling vpon the name of God, & recei-uing of his Sacraments. These causes therefore diligentlye considered, I thought it my duty to dedicate ẏ first fruits of this my labour vnto your ho-nour, partly to declare vnto you mine obedient thanckfulnes of minde, and partlye that both honourable and all others in this lande, beholdinge your honours vertuous and Godlye lyfe, might not onelye imitate and followe the same, but also glorifie God the father of our Lord Iesus Christe. To whom I commende your honour, hartely beseechinge him to encrease in you daily more and more al maner of vertue and godlines, to blesse and enriche you with all maner of prosperity, and to graunt that for our good ensample and to the settinge forth of Gods honour and glorie, you maye liue longe many quiet and happy yeares amongest vs, and after this lyfe, to liue with Christ for euer. Amen,

To his brethren and fellowe Ministers of the Churche of Christe in Englād, the interpretour wisheth peace, & true knowledge, to the honour & glory of God, and to the edification of the sayde Churche, by true vnderstanding and sincere preaching of the worde of GOD.

This little booke intituled Ecclesiastes, and first written in Latyne by Hemminge, was thought meete, and very profitable to be translated, and turned into Englishe, not onely by mee, but also by the iudgement of diuers others of my brethren, godly and zealous Ministers of this citi of London, who cōsidering ŷ great profite that hereby might come, firste vnto the Churche of Christe, and nexte vnto them selues, and to all their other brethren and fellowe Ministers throughout this little realme of Englande, according to their calling, whiche do or ought to thriste and hunger, after the increase and aduauncement of

Christe

Christe his kingdome, to the ouerthrowe & vtter distruction of blindnes, error, Popery, superstition, and of all the tyrannie of Antichriste, haue perswaded me to accomplyshe their great and earnest desire, and to translate into our vulgare tongue, this little and necessary treatise of Himmenge, called Ecclesiastes, wherein what paynes I haue taken, I had rather a great deale the learned in reading should iudge, then that I would speake any one worde of my selfe. This only (as I trust) without offence of any, I maye truely saye, that it would haue bene a great deale easier for me, to haue medled rather with some one whole and continuall commētarie, thē with this little treatise, which in my iudgement may not vnfitly be termed Christiana Rhetorica, that is to say, an arte out of the whiche the true and faithfull Ministers of Christe, may learne playnely, and orderly, to breake and distribute the worde of God vnto the people, and flocke committed to their charge. Nowe it is not vnknowen howe harde a thing it is to translate any arte written, either in the Latyne, or in the Greeke tongue, especially into our Englyshe and vulgare tongue, in the which we haue wordes, neither sufficient, nor yet apte enough to declare & expresse the same: that is to saye, the termes and proper names of arte: as Genus, differentia, species, adiuncta, exordium, enarratio, genus didascalicum, paræneticum. &c. not withstanding this great difficultie whiche might altogether seeme to haue bene sufficient to disswade, hinder, and discourage mee, to haue taken this little harde, and profitable woorke in hande: yet the examples of other wyse & learned men (who before me haue brought into our tongue the artes of Grammer, Logike, Rhetoricke, Arithmeticke, Astronomie, Geographie. &c. did not a little encourage and bolden mee hereunto: so that I thought if other graue, wyse, and learned men, before me, both Romaynes, Italians, Germaines, Frenchemen, and Englishmē, haue thought good for the aduauncement of Philosophie, and humaine knowledge, to bring into their mother tongue those and other like artes firste written in the Greeke tongue, though they could not always finde out proper wordes euery one in their owne tongue to declare ẏ proper termes of arte. I with muche more bouldnes might take in

hande

hand to interprete this little arte of Christian Rhetoricke, especially seing that the same doth so farre passe the arte of Rhetoricke, as ẏ holy worde of God doth excede the knowledge of all manner of humaine philosophie. For that arte doth teache thee, cunningly to handle, & eloquently to speake of worldly thinges, and of mens matters: & that either in prayse, or dispraise, either in defending and prouing, or els in reprouing, impugning, discōmending, and disalowing, wherof we haue examples in Demosthenes, and Ctesiphon, among the Greecians: in M. T. Cicero, and Mar. Antonius among the Romaines, and in diuers other Oratours, who florished in their time. But this doth instructe and teache thee, the true deuision of the scriptures, howe they haue bene diuersly of diuers godlye wryters diuided: What the vse and profite thereof is: what tongues are necessary for thee to learne and vnderstande the scriptures: what the vse of them are. Howe thou must studie diligently and aboue all other writers the holy scriptures. Howe thou must, for thy better vnderstanding, conferre them together, not leauing altogether, either to thyne owne or yet to to other mens opinions: And to conclude, how thou mayst orderly and with profite of thy hearers preache, & expounde the worde of God, whether mẽ are to be lifted vp, and comforted with the swete promises of God, or els to be beaten, and cast downe, with his dreadfull minaces, and threatninges: whether wickednes be to be defaced and troden vnderfoote, or vertue to be praysed, and exhorted vnto: But all these and many suche others, thou shalte more at large better learne out of the treatise it selfe, and therefore I referre thee vnto the diligẽt reading thereof, and do exhorte thee, so to reade, that thou maiest not only hereby learne to know a ready and easy Methode, or wayr of preaching out of the worde of God vnto others, orderly for the helpe both of thine own memorie, and also of thy heareārs: but also, and that especially that with the studye of this arte and Methode, thou alwayes make thy prayers vnto almighty God, for ẏ assistance and helpe of his holy spirite, whiche maye teache thee, the true ende, and right vse of ẏ same. For as arte helpeth nature, & nature arte, so that arte can doe nothing without nature, so must we alwayes remember that the

the Methode or arte of preaching, shall lit‑
tell, or nothing at all profite vs, vnlesse the
the spirite of God bee ioyned thereunto,
whiche is, as it were the true nature vnto
it, and without the which the arte it selfe is
able to doe nothing: for this holy spirite of
God, doth not onely make vs apte, and able
to learne this arte, or Methode, but doth al‑
so teache vs that the true ende, and right vse
hereof, is not onely to preache learnedly, or‑
derly or cunningly the woorde of God vnto
others, but also and that especially vnto our
selues, that our audiēce seing our wise & ho‑
ly sayinges to agre together, with our good
and godly dedes may by our example frame
allso their life, and conuersation according
to our preaching out of the worde of God, &
so to gether with vs both in word and deede
glorifie God the father of our Lorde Jesus
Christe, to whom bee prayse and glory for
euer and euer. Amen.

I haue to desire thee (Christian Reader) to beare with some faultes escaped in the Printing, ẏ which are these as followeth.

Fol.4.pag.2.lin.12. for therfore, reade there are.
Fol.7.pag.1.lin.3. Cathechisis, read Cathecheesis.
Fol.39.pa.1.lin.27.for fractificat, reade fructificat.

The contentes
of this booke.

The

The

The end of the Contentes.

The deuision of the Holy Scriptures.

The holy Scriptures is not after one sorte but diuersly of diuers writers deuided, which thinge ought not to seme straūg, or vnseemelye vnto anye man, for sometines euen of one and the selfe same thinges, there are manye differences according to the diuersity whereof, the diuersityes of deuision may be taken, and authors haue beene accustomed, to appointe such kindes of deuisions, which do seeme to serue best for theyr purpose. Wherefore seinge that the Scripture is diuersly deuided, I will recite in order the chiefe and principall deuisions of the same and wil also declare the vse of them, to the ende that the profite of this varietye and difference may appeare vnto all men.

¶ The first deuision.

The most common deuision of the Scripture is this, whereas it is deuided into the old and newe Testamente, which being ioyned together, are in the Greeke tongue

(by a

by a certaine figure called Antonomasia) named the Bible, which also is therefore sometimes called an Instrumente, because that by it, as by an Instrument, or readye meane, the holy will and woorde of God is broughte and declared unto us. Nowe the Epithetes, or names of old and newe, are taken from the cyrcumstãces of tymes. For it is called the old Testament, because in respecte of the tyme it was the first. Againe it is called the newe, for that according to the time, it was the last. But if any man should thincke this difference to be taken from the diuersitye of couenauntes, it were no great matter: yet the first reason is trewer and fitter for this place. Notwythstanding they which call the olde and the newe Testamente, by the name of bookes, do use the word Testament contrary to the common use.

¶ The subdiuision.

THE olde Testamente is called of the Jewes, [Esrim veorba] and that of his number of Bookes. For they doe receyue xxiiii. Bookes of undoubted aucthority,

which

which they deuide into foure partes, or orders. The first is called of theym Thora, that is to saye, the Lawe or doctrine, and it doth contayne fiue Bookes, to witte Genesis, Exodus, Leuiticus, Numeri and Deuteronomium, which the Grecians call also πεντατευκον, that is to say, A volume contayning fiue bookes. The second parte is called of them Rhesconim Nebiim, that is to saye, the former Prophetes, and this part hath foure bookes, to witte, the booke of Iosua, the booke of Iudges, the booke of Samuell and the bookes of the kinges. The thirde parte is, Acharonim Nebijm, that is to saye, of the latter Prophetes, and it doth comprehende foure bookes, Esaye, Ieremye, Ezechiell, and the booke of the twelue Prophetes, which they call the lesser, as are Osee, Ioell, Amos, Abdias, Ionas, Micheas, Nahum, Baruch, Sophonias, Haggeus, Zacharie, and Malachie. The fourthe parte is Chetubim, that is to saye, of the holye writers, and it doth contayne eleuen bookes, Paralippominon, the Psalter, the Prouerbes of Salomon, Iob, Ruthe, Ecclesiastes, the Lamentation of Ieremye, the Songe of Songes,

Hester, Daniell, Esoras, and Nehemiah, which two latter, are taken for one booke. So that wee haue 24. bookes of the olde Testamente of vndoubted auctority, deuided into 4. partes, or orders. Notwythstãding besides these bookes they haue certaine, also which they do call Apocrypha, that is to saye, secrete or hidden Scriptures, therefore so called, because they were not brought forth into the light, to confirme any opinion or doctrine. Of this sorte are Iesus the sonne of Syrach, Iudeth, Tobias, the bookes of Machabees, the wisedome of Salomon, Baruch, ỳ scribe of Ieremie, and this is the deuision of the olde Testament, after the maner of the Hebrewes and the Gretians.

The new Testamente is deuided into 4. partes. The first contayneth the foure Euangelistes. The second the actes of the Apostles. The third, the 21. Epistles of the Apostles, that is to saye, 14. of Paule, 3. of Iohn, 2. of Peter, one of Iames, and one of Iudas. The fourth part contayneth the Apocalips of S. Iohn. Moreouer all the bookes of the newe Testament, are founde in the Cannon, excepte the seconde Epistle of S.

of S.Peter,the seconde and thirde Epistle of John, and the Epistles of James, and Jude, with the Apocalipse. Some also do put the Epistle to the Hebrewes out of the Cannon.

Now somwhat seemeth to be added,cōcerning the vse and profite of this distinctiō rehearsed: for it little auayleth dilligently to distinguishe, vnlesse thou perceyue also what profite proceedeth thereof. First of all therefore the distinction profiteth much to iudge truly of the auctoritie of Holye bookes: for all the bookes of the olde and new Testament,are of an vndoubted faythe, and are of great force to cōfirme opinions: except those which I sayde before were called Apocrypha, which truly may be reade wyth profite. But in disputations of opinions they are not to be alleaged. For those bookes only are of an vndoubted auctority, which are truly attributed to Moses,to the Prophetes,to the Euangelistes,and to the Apostles. Wherefore since that the Primatiue and pure Church, hath doubted of the auctors of the secrete Scriptures, called Apocrypha, they are of right reiected, when as they are alleaged by the aduersarye against the wrytinges of the Prophets and the Apostles. There is also another commoditie of this distinction, for it is commodious to haue a certain order of bookes, that Students may distribute the reading of the Bible into certayne times, as it shal seeme to be profitable for theym, to learne the holy bookes. The third commoditye is that a certaine waye or meanes maye be had (whether thou preach or interprete the sacred Scriptures in the scholes) of recyting or alledging ye Testimonyes of Scriptures, that the place of the testimonye, may be shewed as it were wyth the finger, when as the aucthour of the wrytinge, and the Chapter of the Booke is named and rehearsed.

¶ The second deuision.

The deuines in the scholes, do deuide the bookes both of the old and newe Testament, into Legall, Historicall, Sapientiall, and Propheticall bookes. As of the olde Testamente, the fiue bookes of Moses are Legall: the bookes called Historicall are Iosua, the booke of Iudges, Ruth, the 4. bookes

bookes of the Kings, Job, the two bookes of the Machabees. The Psalter, ye Prouerbes, Ecclesiastes, the Song of Songes, the booke of Wisedome, Ecclesiasticus, are Sapiential. And the xvii. Prophetes before rehearsed are Propheticall: In like manner also, to the ende theyr ignoraunce might the more euidently appeare, they deuide the bookes of the newe Testamente, so that the bookes of the Euangelistes maye be Legall: the Actes of the Apostles Historicall: the xxi. Epistles of the Apostles Sapiential: and the Apocalipse of S. John to be Propheticall. This by no colour maye bee excused: for it is altogether absurde in as much as it is of them applyed to bookes. But if they woulde applye this theyr subtile deuision to the thinges (as I thincke) auncient wryters haue done, it mighte peraduenture be borne wythall: but because it is manifestlye false, as it is applyed to bookes, I wil not in so euident a matter, make anye longer confutation. Furthermore the vse of this deuision as it is applyed to thinges, perhappes maye be heare in, that learners in readinge maye wyselye put a difference betweene histories and lawes, the Prophetes, and the sayinges of wyse men, that is to say, Gnomas, worthy and approued Sentences.

¶ The third deuision.

The whole Scripture, if thou consider ye thinges subiecte, are fitlie deuided into History and Doctrine, which two the dilligente reader will search oute studiously in reading of holy bookes. Nowe therefore two kinds of Histories, ye old and the newe, the old contayneth all Histories, euen from the beginning of the creation of the world, vntil the conception of our Lord, or the beginning of the Euangelicall historie. This Historye taketh his originall (as I haue said) from the first condition of things, and so continueth vntill the Monarchie of Cyrus. The weekes of Daniel follow after, vntill Christe crucifyed. Moreouer I haue made a computatiō of yeares for memories sake, in these Verses which I will putte downe in Latine,

M.D.C.L.V.I. post Adam mundús inundat.
Post vndas ad Abram, ducent nonaginta duoq;.

Exodus

Exodus hunc sequitur, quingentos quinq; p Annos.
Exodus ad Babylon, nongent, decemq; recenset.
Post Babel ad Christũ, D. & L. tribus, X. datur vnus.

Englished thus.

The world a thousand sixe hundreth fifty sixe yea-
res is found,
After Adam our father by Noes floud drownd.
And from Noes floud to Abram againe,
Wee find two hundred yeares ninety and twaine.
Exodus doth follow him, v. hundred yeres & fiue,
Exodus to Babilon ix. hũdreth and x. cõtriue.
And to our Sauiour Christ from Babilon,
Are fiue hundreth foure score yeares and one.

If thou ioyne these yeares together, thou shalte haue 3944. yeares from the first beginning of thinges, vntil Christes his comminge, the which nomber I am wonte to comprehende in these Verses.

Ter mille, & nõgent, quater, X. duo bis numeratur,
Christus adest nobis, gloria vita salus.

In Englishe thus:

After three thousand nine hundreth 44. yeares,
Christ our glory, life and health to vs appeares.

Furthermore the new history, is discribed

of the

of the Euangelistes, which intreateth of the Conception, Natiuitye Cyrcumcision, Offering, Banishmēt, Disputation, Baptisme, Fastinge, Temptation, Doctrine, Myracles, Death, Resurrection, and Ascention of Christe into Heauen. Also it intreateth of the geuinge of the holy Ghoste in the daye of Penticost, and of the Primatiue Church, and his persecutions: for vnto these Chapters and poinctes, the newe historie shalbe reduced. And thus much cōcerning the Historye.

The doctrine is dispersed throughout al the bookes of the olde and newe Testamēt, and is deuided into doctrine of things, and of signes. The doctrine of thinges is afterwards deuided into the Lawe and the Gospell. The doctrine of signes doth contayne the Ceremonyes and Sacramentes, whereof wee haue heare no time to intreat at large, notwithstandinge the vse of this distinction is not simple, and of one sorte. For the holy historye ought to be the glasse of a Christian lyfe. For it doth contayne many examples of true godlynesse, of confession, of Faythe, of Patience, of calling &c.

It re-

It recyteth the rewardes and punishmentes, both of obedience and disobedience towardes GOD, and comprehendeth manye testimonyes and witnesses of GOD. The difference of doctrine verelye, dothe cause vs not to confounde rashlye wyth the Papistes the Lawe and the Gospell, who dreame the Gospell to be the newe Lawe, but they are deceyued: For neyther the Prophetes, nor the Apostles, teache anye other thinge then Moses doth, althoughe in their manner of teachinge there is great difference. For Moyses committeth to wrytinge the doctrine delyuered, as it were by hande from GOD, and the fathers: whiche doth contayne the perfecte worshippinge of GOD, but hee is more obscure and darke then the Prophetes.

The Prophetes are the interpretours of Moses, for that which Moses doth note, as it were wyth certayne Aphorismes, that is to saye, briefely and summarilye, the Prophetes doe expounde in whole Sermons. But because that thing which the Prophetes did foretell, the Apostles sawe before their eyes, therefore are the Apostles made plainer interpreters of Moses, and of the Prophe-

Prophetes. Who so obserueth this difference, shall reade with greater profite, the wrytinges of Moses, of the Prophetes and of the Apostles. But in what estimation the scholers of the Apostles and other holy interpretours of the Scriptures are to bee had, I will declare hereafter, where I shal intreat of the maner of interpretacion.

¶ The fourth deuision.

There is yet another deuision deliuered or giuen vs by the Gretians, which wee maye not ouerpasse: For the worde of God bringinge saluation vnto mā, is deuided into Protrepticō, that is to say, appertayning to exhortacion: Gnosticon, that is to saye, appertayning to knowledge, Practicon, ꝧ is to saye, appertayninge vnto that whiche they call practise. And vnto that which is called Protrepticon, doe appertaine exhortatiōs, cōsolations, threatnings, chydings, which all are certaine prouocatiōs, or sterrers vppe, to heare the word of God, to embrace and to obey it. Gnosticon, is a part of knowledge which doth cōtayne the worshipping of God, ꝧ knowledge of the Law, of the of the Gospell, and of the Sacraments, the Epitome and briefe summe whereof is Cathechisis, that is to say Instruction. The last appertayneth unto practise, for it is cõuenient that the obedience of the harte, and innocencie of life should follow knowledge: For fayth as S. Paule witnesseth, oughte to be unfayned, and effectual through loue.

This deuision serueth to this ende, that thou maist know the vse of the holy Scriptures, that is to say, that thou mayest obeye the exhorter, beleeue the teacher, and doe according as thou beleeuest. For he is worthy (sayth Agapetus) of God who doth nothing unworthy of God, but thinketh those thinges which are of God, and speaketh the things which he thincketh, & doth the thing which he speaketh.

¶ Of the formes and kindes of Narrations.

In speakinge of the formes of a Narration, I will declare foure thinges in order. First with what helpes he ought to be instructed, that will become a profitable interpretour. Secondly which are the causes of Narrations.

tions. Thirdly what be the kindes of interpreting, and last of all what is the vse of cōmentaryes, or expositions.

¶ The aydes or helpes of an interpretour.

That a profitable interpretour oughte to be instructed with liberal doctrine, and especiallye wyth the knowledge of Rhetoricke and Logicke, there is no man which will doubt thereof. Wherefore I wil come to certaine other helpes by which heede is taken, that the interpretour go not astraye from Godlines. Therefore in intreating of holye misteryes, foure kindes of care especially do belong vnto him, who desireth reth to be free from erroure, and safe from the deceites of hereticks: Let the first care be to seeke God and his will in the Scriptures, wyth feare and humilitie, that hee may knowe him truly in oure Lord Iesus Christe: Let the second care be to haue the sacred worde of God for a rule. This care ioyned wyth the former shall cause thee to be conuersaunt in the Scriptures without arrogancy or contention, and that thou bee not

not puffed vppe wyth foolishe rashnes, but rather craue his helpe with humility, whō in the Scriptures thou seekest faythfully; ẏ seconde care causeth thee also, that thou be not carefull of those thinges which are not founde written in the woorde of the Lorde. For thou oughtest to be content wyth that lighte, which the Lord hath shewed thee to be followed. Let the third care be diligentlye to conferte the Scriptures, to thende that the consente of Moses, of the Prophetes, of Christe, and of the Apostles, maye euidentlye appeare, and that suche sentences as seeme to disagree, throughe conference maye be reconcyled, the cyrcumstaunces of the places beinge dilligentlye obserued. This care causeth thee not rashlye to take houlde of anye one sentence of the Scriptures to assaulte, or repugne another therewyth, from whence no doubt all the sectes of heresye haue spronge vppe, which thing that it maye the more euidentlye appeare, wee shall openlye declare by examples.

Arrius doothe heare the Sonne sayinge: The Father is greater thenne I. This Sentence hee snatcheth, and therewyth

wyth, is girded, and armed to vanquish and ouercome the deuinitie of Christe: Cōtrariwyse, Manichæus to the ende hee mighte take away ẏ humanity of Christ, snatcheth the sayinge of S. Paule in his first Epistle to the Corinthians, the 15. Chapter, where Christ is called the second Adam from heauen heauenlye. Againe there are some which acknowledge the deuinitie, and confesse the humanity, but they make two persons in Christe, the worde, and the sonne of the Virgin. Osiander, because it is written ẏ Lord is our rigteousnes: doth ascribe iustification to the deuine nature alone, as thoughe the humanity were of no force at all, to the benefite of saluation. Stancharus on the contrary syde (because the worde of promise, is of the seede of a woman, and Paule calleth Iesus Christe, beinge man a mediatour) wythdraweth the benefite of redemption from the deuinitie, and doth attribute the same to the onelye humanitye. Here if there had beene ẏ feare of our Lord, and true humilitie, and if the desire of contention and pride had beene absente, they might easily haue iudged of these misteries, by conference of the Scriptures. Let the

first

first care be to referre euery interpretation to the proportion of fayth, from the which if the interpretation doe disagree, it shalbe accompted false. But contrarywise, if it do agree with it althoughe sometimes it erreth from the marke, and minde of the aucthore, yet oughte ye to knowe, that this is done without the danger of saluation. But what is it to call an interpretation to the proportion of fayth? it is so to ordaine it, y^t it maye be corespondente to the first principles of fayth, and that it maye seeme to be as it were builded vppon them. For those thinges are sayde to be done accordinge to the proportion which are made by comparison to another thinge, or els when other thinges are framed by the comparison of others. Whereuppon when Paule doth commaunde that Prophecye, that is to say, the interpretation of the Scriptures, ought to be proportionable to fayth, hee wylleth that the interpretour shoulde haue respecte to the firste principles of Religion, which are plaine and manifest, as conserninge the lawe and the promises of the Gospell, with the which euery interpretation oughte to agree. Wherefore the Papistes in the exposiposition of this saying: (If thou wilt enter into life keepe the commaundementes) Do departe from the proportion of fayth, when they do conclude of this sayinge, That men may obtaine saluation by their owne proper workes, for this interpretation doth striue with cleare and manifest principles: As are these, The seede of the woman shall breake the Serpentes heade, also, The Lambe of God, that taketh awaye the sinnes of the worlde: and againe, If righteousnes be of the law Christe dyed in vaine.

And alwayes after this maner the minde of the interpretour ought to be bent, to the firste principles of our Religion, from the which hee shall not suffer hymselfe to be drawne awaye by any Sophisticall reason: For hee that contemneth this proportion of Faythe, commended of S. Paule to the interpretour, and els where doth seeke an interpretation contrary to the rule of faith, let him be assured that hee shalbe plagued of GOD. For like as in tymes paste vnder the olde Testamente, fyer oughte alwayes to be taken from the fier of the Aulter, wherewith their Sacrifice shoulde be burned: so euery interpretation of ye Scrip-

tures,

tures, should depend vppon the euerlasting word of God. And euen as Nadab and Abihu, for putting straunge fier in theyr Censers, which they were commaunded to doe, were punished of the Lorde: so heretickes bringing in the deuision of reason, and the deceites of Philosophie, in steede of true religion, are to be iudged worthye of punishmente. And thus muche concerninge the helpes of an interpretour: nowe will I declare that which in ye second place was propounded.

¶ The causes of interpretation.

IN ye preface of Philip Melancthons places, foure causes of interpretatiōs are rehearsed, whereof this is the first, yt the kind of speache may be vnderstode: for hearers or readers do not in euery place vnderstand the phrases of a straunge tongue, yea sometimes men of singuler learning take greate paines in this thinge: for oftentimes it happeneth that a sentence being exposided with the word of a straung tongue, which thoughe they aunswering truly in signification, yet notwithstandinge they keepe not the same sence in both tongues, and that for the difference of the phrase, or manner of speache. Therefore least here unwares wee may be deceyued, oftentimes a learned interpretour is needeful. The second cause, is the iudgement of ye order of thinges: For he ye perceyueth not the maner of the handling, shal certainly very oftē times be deceiued: as they are which recyte out of Paule, this saying against ye Iustification of faith: Not the hearers of the Law but the doers shalbe iustifyed. Here if they had considered the maner of the handling they might haue seene Paule in that place, not to haue preached of the iustification of works, yt is to say, yt men shoulde be coūted iustifyed throughe woorkes before God, when as Paule there laboureth to confute this opinion against ye doctrine of fayth. Therefore an interpretour is needeful, which may shew cunningly an order, and the partes thereof: the profite of which thing is greater then that it cā be declared in few wordes. The third cause ought to be the witnes of a true interpretation, for when the hearers perceiue the interpretations to be brought frō the word of God, & do see the agreement of the word of God, and of the pure Church with ye interpretation:

pretation: they loue the doctrine more earnestly, and do learne it more greedely. The fourth cause, is the confutation of false opiniōs, least learners should be infected with the poysons of heretickes. These causes are sufficiently greate enough for ŷ which God wyll haue the mynisterye of his woorde both in scholes, and in Churches to be preserued.

¶ The kinds of interpretinge.

ALthough by those things, which I haue sayd alreadye, concerning the causes of interpretations, the kindes of interpreting may after a sorte be vnderstode, yet because it is needeful to haue them seperated, I wil intreate of them as plainly as I can, accordinge as before I haue promised: wherefore I haue noted foure kindes of expounding holy thinges in reading the commentaryes of diuers aucthours.

¶ The Grammarian his kind of interpreting.

SOme nothinge carefull of the Methode of a treatise, do onely expounde the wordes and ẏ phrases after a familiar & plaine manner, which kinde of interpretation, because it consisteth of a certaine exposition of Grammer, it shalbe called Grammaticall: This kinde did Athanasius, Theophilacte, Ambrose, and many others followe: truly this is prayse worthie, that suche excellente men which were able both aboundantly, & eloquently to make long disputations, and orations of euery matter: that notwithstāding hath submitted themselues, to ẏ Gramariās. For they knew wel that frō thence a true sentence shoulde be taken. Furthermore this kinde of an interpretour, oughte to be instructed with liberall learning. For first he ought to haue the knowledge of that tongue, which ẏ authore of the wryting vseth: vnlesse he desire to see rather wyth other mens eyes thē ẘ his owne. Althoughe a perfect knowledge is not here requyred, yet there ought to be so much skill ẏ hee be able to cōferre together these thre tōgues, the Hebrewe, Greeke and Latin. For a deuine interpretour hath neede of these three tongues, the conference whereof, he that is studious shall perceyue to yeld more profite, then the tedious commētaries of great mē.

Agayne

Againe to thende hee maye interprete that thing aptly, which he understandeth truly, Logicke is necessary, which oftentimes to a Grammarian interpretour, doth put to her willing hand. He shal also be not a litle holpen with the commentaries of variety, frō whence he may learne divers formes of varying one and the selfe same sentence.

¶ The Logician his kinde of interpreting.

OThers when they see, that order obtayneth the chiefest partes in all thinges, they seeke oute and declare the Methode & order of a treatise, & do put forth questiōs, argumentes, collations, and do briefely reduce the argumēts to certaine chapters, or common places, as though they were consultations. This is a most especiall care to this kinde of interpretour, ẏ all things may be expounded openly, and declared distinctlye. But because this kinde is most profitable in the scholes, I will briefely shewe the way, which ẏ interpretour in this kind may safely follow, which thing ẏ it may be done more plainly, I wil cōprehend al the whole matter in foure Canons, or general rules.

¶ The first Cannon.

IN the beginning of y reading of any holy Scripture, he ought first of all things to speake of the kinde of doctrine, and y (as it seemeth to mee) maye fitlye be done after this maner. First, he oughte to expounde what kind of doctrine it is, from whence he may fall into the cōmendation therof. Secōdly, he should shew auctoritie. Thirdly, he should signifye of what certainty it is, & frō whence it should be taken. Fourthly, what is the necessity. Fiftlye, he shoulde declare what profite and cōmodity should procede from thence to the hearers. These fiue pointes in the beginning of any holye booke (in my iudgemente) are verye profitable to be handled. Neither do I disalowe it, if either hee adde some thinges to these, or take other some awaye, so that he deceiue not the hearers, who when they learne, doe also greedelye seeke for the Methode of immitation.

¶ The second Canon.

WHeras according to this first Cannon, we haue generally spoken of the kinde of doctrine, wee may profitablie discende to

Hy-

Hypothesis, that is to say, to the particuler wrytinge, which is layed before vs to be expounded, in which place, these thinges are needefull to bee spoken off, by him which followeth the Logicians kinde of interpreting. First, who and what maner of mã, the aucthour of the wrytinge is, and from whence the aucthoritye of the wrytinge doth depende. Secondly, what was his occasion of wryting, the obseruation wherof helpeth to vnderstande the order of the treatise. Thirdly, what is the state of the matter or principall question, whether one or many from whenc, Judgement may be giuen of the kinde of the cause, and the endeuour of the whole writing, that is to say, the ende and verye laste scope, maye be perceiued and knowne. Fourthly what is the Methode of this present wryting, or (which is all one) what is the order of the treatise, whiche excepte it bee obserued, the laboure of the teacher shalbe little or nothinge profitable.

¶The thirde Canon.

WE must diligently obserue this, in al ỳ writinges of the Prophets and ỳ Apostles,

ſtles, that whilſt they teach, they oftẽtimes fall into admonitions, reprehenſions, prayſes, threatnings, comforts, &c. wherewith they applye their doctrine to the hearers, & do pricke them forwardes, to receiue their doctrine. They that conſider not this, can neither obſerue the order of ẏ treatiſe themſelues, nor yet ſhewe the way well to any others. But I will ſpeake more of this Canon hereafter, wheras I ſhal intreat of the large and ample treatiſe of cõmon places.

¶ The fourth Canon.

AN expoſitiõ of euery chapter may very fitly be made after this maner, in ẏ firſt place the whole chapter muſte be gathered into a certaine briefe collection or ſumme, which none may cõuemẽtly do, vnles he be ſkilful in Logicke. For thoſe things which are ſpoken ſpecially & by parts, he ſhall reduce to generalities & to the whole, and cut of thoſe thinges which are acceſſaries & of leſſe value, neither ſhal he adde to al maner arguments of things, but ſhalbe contẽt only with a ſume of things: and all other matters which are added for amplification, or deduction of thinges muſt be remoued.

In the

In the second place hee shall declare the order of the chapter, in shewing how it agreeth with that which wente before, (if anye thinge wente before) and shall declare the chiefe partes, and giue admonitiō how they follow. In the thirde place the exposition of the texte shall ensue, the common places shalbe noted, that all things may be conuerted to profite. But the waye of the inuention of places, shalbe taughte hereafter, where wee shall intreate of the places that belonge to a preacher: at this time it suffiseth briefely to haue shewed what is needefull to be done.

¶ The oratour his kind of interpreting.

There is also a kind of interpretatiō pertayning to Oratours, most profitable in Churches & scholes, wherein the greateste wits haue exercised themselues: as Basile, Gregory Naziāzene, Chrisostome, Augustine, & many other Greekes & Latins, for these do expoūd euery question more at larg after the maner of Rhethoritians, of which thinge wee muste speake againe when wee come to the treatise of common places.

The

¶ The mixt kinde of interpreting.

The mixt kinde of interpreting is, when ẏ interpretour either mingleth all thinges aboue rehearsed, or els ioyneth certaine of them together, which thing not a few in our time, are wont to do with great profite, in whose nomber Philip Melancthon, wt out doubte is the chiefe, whom manye worthie men: as Bucer, Caluine, Brentius, Beza, & diuers others, do immitate & follow.

¶ The vse of Commentaries.

Many do abuse Commentaries, whilest they labour continually in them, litle or nothing esteeming the text of the Bible, who do like vnto him that trauayling some whither, determineth to abide alwayes in his iourneye. For Commentaries are like to the Image of Mercurie. For like as they are set vp of purpose to shew the right way to trauelers, least they should goe out of the waye, so commentaries do leade, as it were by the hande, the vnexercised reader: which he shoulde not alwayes vse, but so as ẏ trauaylour doth vse the Images of Mercurie. For the trauaylour loketh not vpon them.

when

when by often times goinge that waye, hee knoweth the way perfectly. Here first of all ỹ interpretour is admonished of his dutie, that is to say, that he thincke he oughte to shew a way, and that a most ready waye to the hearers, and not to hinder suche as make hast to go forward. Moreouer euen heare it is euidente in what estimation the disciples of the Apostles, and their successours being interpretours of the Scriptures are to be had. For all these are to be followed in so much as they haue the scriptures of the Prophetes and of the Apostles going before them, but if somtimes they do erre from this, let vs acknowledge our cōmon facility and readines in falling, & pray to God earnestly, that he suffer vs not to fal into daungerous errours.

¶ The waye to frame or make holy Sermons.

The Methode or making of Sermons, is a sure way and meanes shewing a reasō of making sacred Sermons. And because those thinges which are needefull to be declared in the Church, are not of one kinde, nor can be handled after one sorte: It were

verye

verye profitable first to shewe the kindes of Sermons, afterwards the meanes whereby euery thinge maye be intreated of wyth profite, to thend there may be a certaine prescript & compendious way of making Sermons. For such as shalbe ministers of the most holye ministery of the worde (then the which nothing can be more holy) which beinge confirmed with vse and exercise, they may encrease with preceptes of Logicke, & Rhetoricke. I do not forge new precepts, but do applie the common rules of Logitians and Rhetoritians, to a certaine matter, and doe ioyne together with preceptes the practise of learned men, whō I haue heard preache, that the immitation mighte be the more easye, which truly would be but very weake: vnlesse it were holpen wyth preceptes, as I haue said before in the preface.

¶ The kinds of Sermons.

BEfore I come to the kinds of Sermons I will briefely touche the partes, which may very well be counted foure in nomber, the Exordium or beginninge, the Treatise, the Digression end the Conclusion. The

Exor-

Exordium in this place, is the beginning of the sermon, after inuocation and prayer is made, and the holye lesson, or text read and recited, which wee purpose to handle and to intreate of. This may very aptly somtimes be taken vppon the occasion, or oportunity, somtimes from other cyrcumstaunces. And it should be so handled that it might be, as it were a certaine way, to that thing which we minde to intreate of. It must be modest, briefe and graue to thende it maye obtaine the good will of the hearers, maye styrre them vppe by easines of teaching, and maye keepe theym attentiue. The treatise or manner of handlinge, doth alter throughe diuersity of theames, wherby it happeneth that sometimes it is contente with a deuision, and an exposition: and that when it is a simple theame. Diuision is a sentence by the which we briefely declare what things wee will speake of, this is commended for the breuitye, the perfectnes and fewnes of words, for the which aske counsaile & helpe of the precepts of Oratours. Exposition is a sentēce, wherin the parts of a diuision are declared, and it is three fould. Synthetical, Dieretical, and Analyticall, of which here-after

after wee shall intreate more at large. This exposition is sometimes simple, when as no argumentes are added: sometimes mixte, when the reasons of the partes of an exposition are intermingled: sometimes wyth deuision. He may seeke out the confirmation of the partes of deuision, and the cõfutation of the opinions of others stryuing with ours, and that so often as the theame is compounded. The Wysedome of the preacher shal easlye iudge, when the confutation should go before the confirmation, & when it should follow: it must go before of necessitye when the mindes of the hearers are beforehande possessed and holden wyth errour: for they cannot receiue the truth before they are deliuered from the errour and falsehode. Digression is a sentẽce, wherby the doctrine is applyed to ỹ hearers, by cõforting, chiding, fearing & admonishing. In this ỹ beginning, the end, & the place are specially to be cõsidered: the beginning is ỹ it may seeme of his owne accord to flow out of ỹ doctrine. The end ỹ it may go together and agree with the doctrine following, if anye doctrine be expounded: The place ỹ it maye be put to thende of euery member of a de-a diuision or partition, lest the iudgement of learners, should be troubled with interruption of doctrine, more shalbe spoken of digression hereafter. Peroration, is the conclusion of the treatise. This doth both briefly rehearse the summe of the thinges which are handled, and doth also stere vp the mindes of the hearers with the commendation of the doctrine expounded, and by shewyng the vse thereof. Now let vs come to speake of the kindes of a sermon. There are generally twoo kyndes of preachinges, the one appertayneth to teaching: the other to exhortation. That whiche appertayneth to teaching, is of simple places, and those as well of persones as of thinges, and of places compounded, of generall sentences, and particuler argumentes. The other whiche appertayneth to exhortation, is diuided into three partes, for either it persuadeth, or rebuketh, or comforteth. This difference or distinction of sermons may be proued. First of the diuersitie of hearers, to whome the sermon shalbe applied. For either they are altogether rude, and must bee taughte, to whome the first kinde dothe appertayne, or els they are not rude, but rather feble and faint harted, and must be lifted vp with consolations: or els slowe, and they must bee pricked forwarde: or els contemners, and are to be chastened with threatninges. To these foure kindes of hearers al the sermōs of Christe are to be derected, for sometyme hee teacheth the ignoraunt whiche are desirous to learne, and sometime it comforteth, and styrreth vp the faint harted: nowe hee exhorteth the slower sorte, and nowe with threatninges, he terrifieth suche as are prophane, and vngodly. Hereof we may euery-where easelye finde exāples in the historie of the Gospell. Agayne, the same is proued by the vse and custome of the holy Scripture: For Paule wryteth thus in his seconde epipistle to Timothe, and the thyrde chapter. All scripture geuen by inspiration of God, is profitable to improue, to amende, and to instructe in righteousnes that the name of God may be perfecte and prepared vnto all good workes. Here the foure folde vse of the scripture is declared, and that with foure woordes whiche are in the Greeke tongue named Didascalia, Elenchos, Epanorthosis, and Paidia. Didascalia, is to be handled in the first kinde, that is to say, in that whiche apper-

appertaineth to teaching. Elenchos, hath chi ding. Epanorthosis is when the fal is lifted vp, and made stedfast, whiche manifestly appeareth to bee done with consolations and comfortes. Paidia, is the teaching of children, whose chiefest office is, to perswade to goodnes, and honestie, and to dissuade from wicked and filthie thynges. Our distinction therefore agreeth with the varietie of the hearers, with the ensample of Christe, and with the tradition of Paule. But because the hearers are mixed in publicke assemblies it cometh to passe, that the prophetes, Christ, thapostles, & all the godly ministers of the worde doe oftentimes builde & frame out of doctrine, consolations perswasions, and chidings, all which the force of doctrine hathe as it were ioyned with it: euen as I haue sayde before, is done in the wrytinges of the Prophetes and Apostles: whose examples it becommeth godlye ministers to folowe in makyng of Sermones. Neyther is our distinction to bee disallowed whiche doth appertayne to the nature of teachynge of thynges, and doth shewe what order and waye is to be obserued in makyng of Sermones, although sometymes those thynges whiche I haue named as accessaries, and impertinent, are applied by the figure of digression, which thing who so euer doth not obserue, can neyther make their owne sermons well, neyther iudge of other mens, nor yet beare them awaye in mynde. Wherfore the kyndes of sermons must first be distinguished, and then those thinges whiche are added, maye verye well bee formed and framed.

¶ The kynde of teaching.

That part of sermon which appertaineth to teaching, is that whose ende is, to teache the ignoraunte hearers. In this kynde of sermon the godly preacher shall imploye his whole strengthe first that he himselfe do perfectly vnderstande the thing that is to be taught: Next that hee frame with him selfe a full and perfecte order of the same in wryting. Thirdly, that hee expounde the same in a plaine and common speache, not hauing any respecte to his owne commendation for his eloquence, but rather to aduaunce the glory of God, and helpe the capacitie of the present hearers, whiche if hee doe, he may hope that the hearer shall not wauer in opinions any more, but conſent to the true and cleare doctrine. And becauſe there are two kyndes as before in diuiſion I haue declared, that ſermon which appertaineth vnto teaching, to wytte, Simple or of ſimple places: and compounde or of compounde places: The order of teaching requireth that in the firſt place, wee ſpeake of the ſimple manner of teaching, but becauſe in the ſimple kind of teaching, ſometimes the perſons, ſome times the thinges are intreated of, it ſeemeth beſt firſt to ſpeake of the treatiſe of perſons.

¶ Of the ſimple kinde of teaching which belongeth vnto perſones.

There are twoo kindes of the treatiſe of perſones, the one belõgeth to examples the other vnto demonſtration. For if anye deede of the perſone is layde before vs, it is an example: but if the whole perſone be diſcribed it is ἐπιδειξις, that is to ſay, demonſtration of the perſone.

Of that treatiſe of perſons whiche belong to examples.

When any persone therfore is set before vs out of the holy histories, whose whole life is not described, but some deede of yͤ persone is brought forth, & that for the cause either of the doctrine, or of yͤ immitatiõ, or els of the admonition, it shalbe a treatise Paradigmatical, yͭ is to say, belonging vnto exãples. After this mãner Paule doth set forth Abraham to the Romaines, & to the Galathians, after this manner the epistle to the Hebrewes, chap. xi. reciteth a great scroule, & number of prophets & of kings. By Abrahã his deede, the doctrine & nature of faithe is taught, the immitation cõmended, yͤ exercises of vocation, & the fruites and workes of true godlines are cõfirmed. The repẽtaũce of Manasses doth teache vs yͭ such as do fal, are receiued againe, & therfore is profitably set before vs for immitatiõs sake: it putteth vs in minde of yͤ mercy of God, which of his mere goodnes, receiueth into fauour so cruell a persecutour of his churche, & so vile an Idolater. But here we must speake against those men, who oftentimes do abuse the exãples of sainctes For there ar some who had rather immitate yͤ wicked deedes of saincts then their vertues: & do defend thẽ selues wͭ the exãples of sainctes. There are some also

whiche

which out of the personal deedes of saínctes and extraordinary cōmaundements, do sīsa uoredly frame a forme of an act, & do cōmēd the same as a generall lawe: they are not worthy of any answer. These ar to be called againe into the right way by an admonitiō. For it behoueth vs to kepe a difference betwene ẏ cōmon & personal cōmaundemēts, or precepts of godlines, which only do touch one people, or one mā. The Hebrewes were cōmaunded to robbe the Egiptiās. Abrahā by Gods cōmaundement maketh him selfe ready to slaye his sonne, for a sacrifice in the moūte Moria. These personal actes are not to be applied particularly, but onely generally: For out of both these exāples we must learne obedience vnto God in those thinges which he requireth of vs in his worde. Also in this treatise of the exāples of persons, it is manifest, ẏ the papistes, & especially ẏ mōkes haue daūgerously erred: who ī their sermōs haue laide before vs I know not what counterfait petie saínctes, & haue fained them to haue liued al their life long so blameles, ẏ they neuer offēded, no not in the least thing. Such a fained descriptiō of persōs, maketh rather to disperatiō thē to ẏ edifieng of ẏ cōscience, wrastling ẇ the greatnes of sinne, & of the wrath of God. Ther-

Therfore let vs take vnto vs true examples, and let vs leaue fayned examples for the Poetes, whiche are not to be handled of thē whiche are called by saint Paule the Stewardes of the misteries of God. The sacred scripture and the true historie doth minister examples sufficiently: as of Abraham, Iob, of Ioseph, of Manasses, of Mary Magdalene, of the theefe which was cōuerted, & of such like: for out of such as these ar, we may not onely teache the hearers true godlines, but also ẏ forme of liuing according to their kynde of calling. Therfore the godly preacher must remember to shewe forthe examples profitable vnto godlines, and not those whiche seeme to cause disperation. Nowe it is time that we declare those thinges wherof wee haue spoken with a playne example. And because none can be more famouse thē the example of Abraham, I wil lay that before you to be examined. Paule sayth, Abraham beleued God, and it was imputed to him for righteousnes. In this place Paule bringeth forth the example of Abraham, especially for doctrines sake, and from thēce draweth foorth not only the firme and sure doctrine of righteousnes, but also ẏ nature of of faith: and frō thence doth shewe of what holines of life the beleuing man oughte to be. After this manner let vs learne, by the immitatiō of Paule to obserue two thinges in examples to witte, the facte in it selfe, and then the circumstances of the persone, and of the facte. The facte in it selfe doth teache that true righteousnes doth consist of faith, in the promises of God. The circumstances of the persone, and of the facte, doe put vs in minde of many thinges. First that Circumcision of necessitie is not required to iustification: For Abraham was iustified before Circumcision, but afterwards circumcision was added, as a seale of righteousnes which is of faith. Secondly, the profession of Abraham, his life before iustificatiō, witnesseth ẏ he was receiued of God, not for his owne proper merites, or workes going before, but by the onely goodnes of God. Thirdly, in this example of Abraham is declared that iustification of faith, pertaineth equally to all. For Abraham was iustified before men were discerned by any outward workes. Out of this circumstance the Prophets without doubt haue drawen and framed their sermons, of the callinge of the Gentles.

Gentiles. Fourthly, that the ceremonies of Moyses are not required of them that are to be iustified: for euen as Abraham was iustified without them, so they that shalbe iustified after his example, must not require them to the accomplishement of their iustificatiō. Fiftly, that righteousnes doth come without the morall lawe, and the workes commaūded in the decaloge or two tables, for if we be iustified according to Abraham his example, & he was iustified many yeares that is to say, 430. yeares before the lawe: truly it can not bee that righteousnes is of the lawe. But if any mā should obiecte that the morall lawe was from the beginning, & that Abraham did not wante it, the answer is easye: for no rewarde is due to workes without the couenaunt of God. For workes are not meritorious of their owne worthynes, but by the acceptation of God and by reason of the couenaunt: Therefore the cōclusion of Paule abideth firme and stedfast: Abraham is iustified by the fayth of promise before the couenaunt of woorkes was published: to wytte, the man that dothe them shall liue in them. Wherefore he is iustified by fayth & not by workes. Sixtly, that the true

true and iustifieng fayth, is a certayne full assuraunce, whiche is not subdued by argumētes of reason, but stedfastly beleueth that he whiche promyseth cannot lie, how soeuer the whole nature of thynges may seeme to gayne saye it. And that fayth hath good workes, and obedience towardes God ioyned with it, and that nothing ought to bee estemed dearer to a Christian man, then to be obedient to the will of God. And so the Prophetes, godly kynges, Apostles, and in like manner all godly men after Abraham, first by example haue learned the true waye of iustification, and afterwardes by the circumstaunces of the persone, and the facte, haue bene admonished of moste weyghtye things. By this meanes the godly preacher by the example of Paule, may applye other examples, both in them selues and also in the varietie of circumstaunces, and all ways in his application, he must remēber to haue a regarde to the proportion of fayth.

¶ Of that kynde of treatise of persones whiche belongeth to demonstration.

The

That kynde of treatise of persons whiche belongeth unto demonstratiō doth handle the whole life, and also euery parte of ẏ life of any persone, and that in the same order, as the places of persones are rehearsed in the questions of Philip Melancton. For that order is not only naturall but also profitable to the speaker and to the hearer. But first of al this is to be obserued in this kinde of treatise of persones, that those members especially are to bee adourned, and beautefied, from whome these three aboue rehearsed, doctrine, immitation, & admonitiō may be taken. For Paule in the. xv. chapter to the Romaines, doth admonishe vs of this of application, when he sayth: what soeuer thinges are written, are writtē for our learning. &c. Therefore suche members ought to be applied to the whole body of ẏ church whiche thing is done when wee transferre aright the particuler to the generall sentences: as if the life of John Baptiste, were to be handled after the manner of demonstration: to obserue the naturall order, wee should intreate of his parentes, of his conception, of his natiuitie, of his education, of his vocation, of his office, of the testimonie of of Christe, of his death and of those thinges that happened both about & after his death. In the member of his parẽtes, these things are contained, that the continual prayers of all godly are heard at the length, that the afflicted whiche beleue do obtayne comforte at the laste, and that God dothe allowe the marriage of priestes. In the member of his conception first the office of Aungels is to be considered, that they are the Embassadours of God, & the ministers of ẏ churche. Secondly, that God is myndefull of his promises. Thirdly, that the power or worke of God is not hindred by naturall impediment, that is to saye, through barrennesse & wante of nature. Last of all, because Iohn as yet in his mothers wombe did acknowledge Christe, it teacheth vs, that children are receyued of God, and that God wyll be acknowledged & honoured of children. In the member of his natiuitie, thankefulnes towardes God, for his benefites receiued is commended, the mutuall office of the godly is shewed, that they ought to reioyce with them, on whom God poureth his blessing: & to conclude, that the godly ought to bringe and offer their children vnto God. Againe

his

his straightnes of life doth commende unto us, not a monkishe or solitary lyfe, but sobrietie and obedience unto God. After all these things in his office, & in the circūstaūces of his persone, and office, not onely his doctrine, but also his consolation, his constācie in his office, his confession, his crosse, and loue of the truth, with other innumerable vertues are set forth unto the godly His cōfort or consolation, is in that he did shewe, or point out wͭ his finger our sauiour Christe: his constancie in that cōtemning the threatninges of Herode and of the Pharisels: hee taught the Gospell without any feare: his confession, in that he confessed him self to be the voyce of a crier in the wyldernes. His crosse, in that according to his vocation, hee did not onely wander abroade without any certayne mansion place: but also doubted not to suffer death. All these thinges which are so drawen forth of the circumstaunces of the persone and of his office, are first layd before godly ministers of the worde, for the cause of doctrine, of immitation, and of admonitiō, and afterwardes generally to the whole uniuersall churche, so farre forth as it belongeth to the common duties of godlines.

lines. For personall factes are not to be applied specially, but generally, as I haue declared before. There is an other kynde of handling examples, to wytte, when the respecte of order and of times is not had, but only certaine vertues and vices are rehearsed, and set foorth at large, but this waye is to be referred, to that kynde of treatise of persones, whiche belongeth vnto example. And thus muche spoken of the two kyndes of the treatyse of persones, whereof the one belongeth to exāple, & the other to demonstration, shall suffice. Nowe the way of drawyng forth places, by whiche the examples are applied to the Churche, shalbe handled afterwarde, where as wee shall entreate of the finding out of the common places. In this place suffiseth to haue the methode, and in fewe examples to haue declared the vse thereof.

¶ Of that simple teaching which belongeth vnto thinges.

The simple kynde of teaching whiche belongeth vnto thinges (that is to saye) as they commōly terme it, of simple places, is when

when the hearer is to bee instructed of one simple thing: as of God, of sinne, of grace, and of Christian iustificatiõ. &c. This forme requireth a more perfect way of handling, and hath neede of greater workemanship. And albeit this methode properly cõsisteth of an exposition euen as the compound doth of argumentation, yet the members of this fourme shalbe confirmed by argumentatiõ. Therefore the instrument of the present fourme, is properly exposition: But argumentation is added, to supporte and helpe the partes of exposition. And furthermore, this is to be obserued, that in this fourme a threefolde exposition is wont to be added, to witte, a Diereticall, a Sintheticall, and an Analyticall, for otherwyse an other way is more fitter.

¶ Of the simple kinde of teaching of thinges by a figure called Diæresis, that is to saye, diuisiou.

ALthough the Diereticall order (whose chiefe members are difinition, and diuision) of handling simple thinges, is both of Philippe Melancthon in his Methode of simple

simple teaching, and also of other Logiciãs diligently declared: yet I thinke it profitable in this place, to prescribe a waye of intreating, whiche shalbe commodious to newe beginning preachers. First therefore I will set downe the chiefe chapters, and next declare the Methode of the of the treatise. The chapters or chiefe pointes ar these,

1 Definition.
2 Diuision or partition.
3 Causes.
4 Effectes.
5 The vse and the abuse.
6 Contrarieties.

¶Of definition.

Of definition some are ours, and some ar our aduersaries. Those which ar ours, we must expounde as true, we must proue, confirme, and gather together: The others we must confute as false. In bothe kindes there is a peculier Methode, but first we wil speake of the former. The definitiõ therfore wich the godlye preacher shall declare as true and immouable, must haue foure parts in the treatise, Exposition, Reason, Confirmation & conclusion. Exposition is a sentēce wherby we expounde our own diffinition of any thing with manifest & playne woordes. And there is two kindes of definitiōs, pertaining to a deuine, the one short & briefe, ỳ other copiouse & large, that is content with the kinde & with the difference. This doth applie to the kinde, & to the differēce, causes, things adioyning, or annexed proprieties, & sometimes circumstaunces.

The reason is the proofe of the definition. Confirmatiō, is that wherby we confirme & declare the reason, either by examples, or by any other manner of declaration.

Conclusion is a briefe comprehension of ỳ exposition of the reason, & of the confirmation. Furthermore, I would haue ỳ whiche is spoken of the reason, & of the confirmatiō to be so vnderstanded, not that a simple reason, or a simple confirmation onely, but that also both many reasons, & cōfirmatiōs, may bee added, as shall seeme profitable to the hearers, & to the thing ỳ is to be intreated of. Furthermore, this is to be obserued, that a large definition which is to be cōfirmed, & proued, must first bee resolued into propositions, somtimes also into boūdes or termes,

then

then afterwardes by litle & little, ye partes must be ioyned together by cōposition, & the necessitie of the definition must be shewed: & all these are to be added to the māner & way of definitiō. Now by one or two exāples, let vs make our preceptes manifest, & let vs take Matrimonie in hande, for to be first of all defined. Matrimonie is a lawful cōiunction of a man & womā (this is the expositiō of the definitiō ye reason followeth) for it is writtē, wherfore let ye man forsake father & mother and cleaue vnto his wife (the cōfirmation foloweth) if these wordes were truly examined, we should finde in them, ye which we did put in the definition. For first they testifie that there ought to be a coniunctiō which is lawful, when it is done according to ye word and will of God. Furthermore where as he saith: they shalbe two in one flesh, he would haue the copulatiō of one man & one womā, not of one husband & many wiues, neither of one wife & many husbandes, euen as the first wedlocke of Adam and Eue doth witnes & declare vnto vs. (Complexion foloweth.) Therfore since God hath cōmaūded by his own law ye two persōs should be lawfully coupled together, & ye there should bee no mo persons in matrimonie thē two. It foloweth that Matrimonie is a lawfull cõiunction of man & wife: By this exãple the treatise of a simple definition may after a sort be vnderstanded, whiche if thou wilt applie to the lawes & rules of Logicke, the first parte is called the question: the second, the reason, the thirde the confirmation of the reason, or the shewynge of the cause of the reason: the fourth is the conclusion, wherin by a particular forme the reason is repeated with the question. Notwithstãding the names of the members whiche I haue aboue rehearsed, do serue rather the popular & vulgar treatise, & are more easy to be vnderstanded Let vs also adde an other example, of a large definitiõ, which we wil declare more at large. And let vs take the Gospell to bee defined. The Gospell is a doctrine reuealed from God, wherin deliueraunce frõ sinne, & from the curse of the lawe, & the wrath of God is preached & remission of sinnes, saluation, & life euerlasting is proclamed, to al beleuers in the sonne of God for his sacrifice, that the goodnes and mercie of God towardes men might be preached, and that being deliuered by ẏ sonne, they might declare forth fruites worthy of the Gospell. Thus farre goeth the

the exposition of the definition, whiche is to be resolued by resolution into these propositions, whereof the first is ỷ the Gospell is a doctrine reuealed frō God. The second, that the Gospell doth declare deliuerance from sinne, frō the curse of the lawe & the wrath of God. &c. The third, that it proclaimeth remissiō of sinnes, saluation, & life euerlasting. The fourth, that those benefites happen to them that beleue in Christ. The fift that the force of the Gospell doth rest in the sacrifice of Christe. The sixt, that out of the Gospell God is to be preached. The seuenth, that man oughte to shewe his thankefulnes to God, in godly liuing. These propositions must be in order cōfirmed. The reason therfore of the first proposition doth follow, that the Gospell is a doctrine reuealed frō God. Paule doth teache manifestlye calling the Gospell a secret misterie, frō the beginning of the world. (The confirmation) by whiche wordes he teacheth openly, that the Gospel dependeth not of mans reason. For if reason by any meanes were able to knowe this doctrine of his own strēgth, it had not bene called a secrete misterie from the beginning of the worlde. (The reason of the seconde proposition (furthermore that deliueraunce from sinne, from the curse of the lawe, and the wrath of God is declared in the Gospell many testimonies of the Prophetes and of the Apostles do teach vs. Daniel saith plainly that Christ shal take away sinnes. Paule teacheth that the curse of the lawe is abolished by Christ his cōming. The father crieth from heauen that he is pleased by his sonne. (the confirmation) that this is true al godly men haue experience, hauing the testimonie of the holy ghost, by whome they crie Abba father, whiche certainly they would not do, vnlesse they did stedfastly beleue that sinne is taken away, the curse of the lawe abolished, the wrath of God pacified, (the reason of ye third proposition) furthermore y^t^ the remission of sinnes, saluatiō, & life euerlasting, is proclaimed in the Gospel, these testimonies beare witnes. The lorde himself saith, it is thus written, that repentaunce & remissiō of sinnes ought to be preached in his name, the same preaching beginning at Hierusalē. In the last of saint Marke saluatiō is promised to all beleuers. Likewyse in the x. chap. to the Romains: Furthermore the lorde him self doth promise euerlasting life to al them that

that beleue in him. what nedeth many wor-des. The vniuersall scripture doth promise remission of sinnes, saluation & euerlasting life, to al people embracing the Gospel. (the confirmatiō.) For it cannot be chosen, but y^t the wrath of God, the curse of ye law, & sinne being taken away: saluatiō, righteousnes, & life must needes bee obtained. But because these things happē not to al men. For Caine Iudas, Saule, & many others haue perished, & at this day a great part of the world (a grief to heare) do fal into euerlasting destruction. In the definitiō fourthly is added y^t these be-nefites do happen to them y^t beleue (the rea-son) for the lord saith plainly, he y^t beleueth in me, shal not perishe, but haue euerlastiug life. (The confirmation) and lest any man should thinke that this doth depend vpō the condition of workes, Paule wryteth that a man is iustified by faith without workes, & with lōg disputatiōs cōfirmeth the same in his epistle both to ye Romains, & to ye Gala-thians. Moreouer in the fift place is added, that the force of the Gospel doth consiste in the sacrifice of Christe, (the reason) for so Paule sayth: by the redemption whiche is in Christe Iesus (The comprobatiō) for the worde which Paule vseth here is Apolytrosis, that is to saye, redemptiō which is done when by death the price is payd. For Lytrō properly is the price of redemption. Such a price Christe payd for vs whē he was made sinne for vs, that we may be made the righteousnes of God. In the sixt place, is added that God should be preached for his goodnes & mercy, (the reason) whiche thing the multitude of Angels do sufficiently proue, & conuince, singing this himne to God, at our Lordes birthe, Glorie be to God on high, & peace on the earth, & vnto men good will. (The confirmation) for we ought to thinke that this thing done therfore ẏ al mē which do acknowledge this Christ, may learne by the exāple of the Angels, to preache ẏ goodnes & mercy of God, especially when nature it selfe doth crye out & teache vs, ẏ thankes ought to be geuē for benefites, or good turnes. In ẏ last place, is added ẏ fruites which they ought to shew, who are deliuered by ẏ Gospel (ẏ reason) which thing is confirmed by the testimonie of Paule, saying wee are created in Christe Jesus to good workes, in the whiche the Lorde woulde haue vs to walke (the Confirmatiō) for how may these twoo two agre that we are deliuered from sinne, and yet fulfill the desires of sinne, when Paule affirmeth that the healthfull grace of God appeared to all men, that we denying vngodlines and worldly lustes, shoulde liue godlye, soberlye and righteously. &c. Seinge therefore that wee haue shewed by stronge reasons, that sinne, the curse of the Law, and the wrath of God is taken away by the Gospell, and that in theyr place doe succede Righteousnes, Saluation and life thorow Christe, which whilst wee beleue in him, and that God would that wee shoulde preach his goodnes for this his benefits, & in all our life time be thanckfull: that followeth which before we propounded that the Gospell is a doctrine reuealed from God, wherein is shewed. &c. Now when our definition is after this maner handled, if there be any of a contrary opinion, they are to be confuted with the Methode of confutation, which consisteth of proposition, sublation, the opposite, contrarye, or proposition, and the solution. The proposition in this place is the promise of the sublation, sublation is the proposition of our aduersaries. The opposite proposition, is the promise of the solution.

tion. The solution is the confirmation opposite proposition. But the matter shalbe made manifest, by a briefe exāple. Neither am I ignoraunt that oure aduersaryes the Papistes, do bable (this is the proposition of the confutation, sublation foloweth) that the Gospel is the new law of not reuēging, of casting awaye of ryches of not swearinge &c. The opposite proposition foloweth, but how vaine a thing that is, may easely be declared (the solution followeth:) For that which they affirme is directlye against the sacrifice of Christe, yea and against ỹ whole Scripture, which plainly sheweth that we obtaine the benefits of the Gospel by fayth. What? are not Paule his woordes manifest? If righteousnes be by the law, Christ dyed in vaine: this confirmation of the opposite proposition is to be taken oute of the places of confirmation, that is to say, out of the places of Logicke, of which thing I wil speake in the compoūd Methode of places. But what generally both in confirmatiōs, and confutations is to be obserued, heare those ỹ are studious are to be admonished. First therefore after that wyth manifest & plaine arguments, thou hast confirmed the concōtrary proposition in order, the argumēts of our aduersaryes are to be refelled, and if the matter suffer it so to be, firste of all the first kind is to be taken, and afterwards we must come to the speciall arguments: as in this presente cause. First wee must confute this that the Gospell is a Law. Secondlye that it is not a law of forbidding of reueng, of castīg away of riches, of not swearing &c. Furthermore this also both in the cōfirmation of our owne opinion, & in the confutation of the contrary part is diligently to be noted and marked, that thou preuent those thinges which eyther the wisedome of the fleshe or els the contrary part may obiecte against those things which thou sayest and confute them. This seemeth to be oftentimes vsed of Paule in his wrytinges, as in this confutation layed before vs of ỹ opiniō of ỹ Papistes, ỹ the Gospell is ỹ new Law: the flesh vnthanckful to God, frō thence taketh weapons vnto himselfe against the doctrine of works, & inferreth or cōcludeth after this maner: If the Gospel doth deliuer vs wout our workes, wherefore should wee worke well? This obiection is to be taken away by preuention. And after this maner

the faith

the faythfull preacher must haue a respecte what maye be sayd on the contrary part. But the preceptes of a large confutation, & confirmatiõ, are to be handled afterwards.

¶Of Diuision and partition.

This member of the Methode may be hãdled verye profitablie after this maner. First if thou expounde thine owne diuision, or partition. Secondlye if thou proue it. Thirdly if thou cõfirme it. Fourthly if thou gather it againe together. Let this be ẏ example of diuision: wee haue heard what the Law is, it remayneth now that wee declare into how many parts it is deuided (for such a forme of transition is to be vsed, when we go from one thing to another.) The Lawe of God therefore is three folde, Morall, Ceremoniall and Judiciall. This was the exposition (The reason) For all the Lawes of God eyther teacheth manners, or commendeth Ceremonies, or practiseth iudgemẽts. (The confirmation) for by these mans life is very well conserued and gouerned. For in a ciuill life there is neede of iudgements, in the publicke assemble of the Church Cerimonies are necessary, and that religion of the minde towardes God, and godlines towardes men (in the spirituall kingdome of God) do consist in the preceptes of maners It is most euident (the collection) Therefore that is most sure which we haue sayd, that the Lawe of God is threefold, Moral, Ceremoniall, and Judiciall. Especiallye since the true gouernment of lyfe consisteth of these three, whether thou consider the common life, or the Church or the spiritual kingdome of God. If these members of diuision be darcke and obscure, they are to be expounded by definitions, and subdiuisions, & are to be made manifeste by reasons and examples. But if the aduersary do obtrude or bringe in any other diuision that is false, it is to be ouerthrowne by ẏͤ Methode of cōfutation. There needeth no ensamples in a manifest thing. Moreouer partition, is to be framed after the same sorte. As the parts of repentaunce are, contrition, faith, and a desyre to leade a godly life: (the reasō) for it becōmeth vs to be sory for our sinnes, and because the contrition is of no force vnlesse there be also fayth in Christe, this is of necessity requyred. And because neither of these

these is true, vnlesse the desire to liue a good and godly life doth follow, a good purpose of necessitye is ioyned with the former (the comprobation) for wee see both the Scriptures and the examples do ioyne these three together: Dauid being fallen was sorye ẏ he had sinned, he fled by fayth to mercy, and the rest of his life withall the endeuour hee might be kept innocente. These members of partition if they be ioyned wyth definitions, deuisions and their reasons, a greate, profitable, and plentiful Oration wil ensue and arise thereof.

¶ Of causes.

NOw we must ad ẏ causes of a thing altogether after a naturall order, & must seclude or set a part those thīgs which seme to be the causes of a thinge, and yet are not. To euerye kinde of cause their reasons are to be added out of the word of the Lorde. Compounded causes do runne together in their actions, and doe stande with mutuall helpes, and euerye one hath a certaine proprietye in actions. Wherefore the orders of causes are diligentlye to bee considered, least there shoulde be a confusion of causes,

from

from whence afterwardes great darcknes might aryse. Furthermore this is also to be obserued, when any thing is commaunded or forbidden, al coordinate causes are commaunded and forbidden. As whē the sanctification of the name of God is commaunded, which cannot be withoute Fayth, neyther without the knowledge of God, which knowledge of God cannot be withoute the preachinge of the worde of God. Therefore when wee are commaunded to praye for the sanctification of the name of God, wee aske and praye for these thinges in order, for the preaching of the word, for the knowledge of God, for Fayth, and for the sanctification it selfe of the name of God. Nowe I will brieflye shew an example hereof. The causes of repentaunce are not the free will of man (this is the seperation) but firste the worde of God, next the holy Ghost, who inwardlye reproueth sinne, & stirreth vp a hatred of sinne in the harte of man, and last of all a will not resistinge the deuine motion, and the worde. The endes are the glorye of God, and the saluation of the penitente personne. These are compounde causes, and doe stande wyth mutuall helpes in their theyr actions, and it easelye appeareth that euerye of them hath a certaine propriety in theyr order to the effect . Moreouer, how these are to be declared by definitions, and confirmed by testimonies, maye by the former preceptes be vnderstanded.

¶ Of the effect.

The effects are to be expounded, proued, confirmed and gathered to gether, and they which are attributed to a thing falsly, are to be ouerthrowne by the Methode of confutation. As if a man shoulde affirme ẏ contrition deserueth remission of sinnes, he is to be confuted after the same manner, as before I haue declared.

¶ Of the vse and abuse.

If the thing haue bene abused, first the abuse muste be confuted by the Methode of confutation. Secondlye the true and righte vse, muste be expounded proued and confirmed.

¶ Of contarries.

Contraryes haue no certaine place, neither in this Methode, nor in others, but are to be dispersed heare and there, for illustration and amplifications sake. For Rhetoricians do thincke that nothing maketh a thing so plaine and easye, as the conferring of thinges which are contrary.

¶ Of the simple kinde of teaching called Sintheticall.

The Sintheticall exposition is, when we begin with those thinges that go before the matter, and by little and little, by certaine steppes and degrees do put them together, and lay them on a heape, until al those thinges do seeme to be gathered, which are sufficient to discusse the nature of the thing: As if we should intreat of that peace which we haue in God by fayth, these things may be expoūded by the figure called Synthesis, that is to say, composition. First we must declare what the offence is. Secondlye the partes of the offence. Thirdly the mediatour. Fourthlye the recompence and satisfaction of the iniurye and hurt. Fiftly the reconsiliation. Sixtlye the couenaunt of reconciliation. Seuenthly the declaration, or publishing of peace. Eightly the fruites of peace. If these were proued one after another, cōfirmed and examplifyed by testimonyes and examples, there would spring and arise a large and plentifull Oration. On this wise Synthesis doth followe the order of nature, and findeth out, expoundeth, proueth and confirmeth all those questions, ỿ naturally go before, and doth by cōtraries, examples, similitudes, and dissimilitudes, examplifye them. Furthermore this also is to be obserued that large and plentifull definitions by this Methode are made and framed, as before ye may see in the definition of the Gospell.

¶ Of the simple kinde of teaching called Analyticall.

The Analyticall exposition is when wee begin from the whole, or from the ende, and afterwards finde out the partes, & those thinges which are required to the ende by an order, cleane contrary to the former, as if we shoulde intreate of prayer in this Methode, wee must expounde what inuocation is is (for a definition contayneth the reason of the whole) and what is the ende thereof: After that we must number and coũt those thinges which appertaine to prayer, as though they were necessary members therof, as are the affections of the minde, the causes, wherefore wee praye, who is to be prayed vnto, by whom, and what wee must praye for. Which for memoryes sake, I am wont to comprehende in this litle Verse:

Affectus causæ, quis, per quem quidq;, petendum.

That is to saye: In prayer these thinges are chiefely to be obserued.

Affections, causes, who, by whom, and what is to be asked.

Last of al indifferent circumstances may be added: as the indifferent circumstaunces of prayer, are place, time, and gesture. If these trulye were proued and made manifest: by the Scriptures, and by examples, a greate and profitable copie of Oratiõ would grow thereof. Moreouer, what so euer wee haue hyther to spoken of the simple treatise of thinges, or places, ought so to be vnderstãded, ỹ they ought al to be done according to the artificial maner of diuers Methodes, of simple questions. But because varietye delighteth them that are exercised, some times learned Preachers do not follow the lawes of this Methode exactlye, but do call the hearers as it were to counsell, and to chuse those thinges of greate plenty, which they thinke most profitable for to be known of the presente hearers. And this reason of intreating of thinges, some do call the Methode of Prudence, which considereth the weight of thinges and the cyrcumstaunces of the present hearers. As if a man woulde intreate of the Lawe of God. Heare first he should behould the hearers, and then consider the waighte of the thinges, and then he should more easely reduce the treatise vnto a fewe Chapters, easye to be vnderstoode & borne awaye. And firste perchaunce hee should expound what the Law is: Secondlye whether any man may fulfil the Law of God: Thirdly what is the vse thereof whē no man fulfilleth it: Fourthly what maner of abrogation of the Lawe is to be vnderstanded. The like maye bee done in other simple questions. And althoughe these thinges be so, yet shall the Methode of this art which I haue expoūded, profite the new preachers which are not as yet practised, &

that

that both to strengthen their memorie, and also bringe longe time and muche practised therein, that they may afterwards luckely folow both kindes. Philip Melancthon of most holye memorye, applyinge himselfe to the common capacitye of men in the explication of any simple matter, iudgeth that these foure are to be propounded, declared, and amplifyed. The definition of the thing, the causes, the partes, and the duties. The definition being drawne out of the cōference of manye sayinges, and noble examples, dothe gather the whole matter as it were in one bundle, and propoūdeth briefly the summe of the matter: the explication of causes doth fortifye the definitiō, the rehersal of partes doth more distinctly set the nature of the thinge before our eyes. In the worde offices, the vse, the effectes, and the finall causes of the thinge are comprehended

Moreouer this is also to be admonished ẏ in handling of places, whether they be simple or compounde, if there be many places, wee muste diligentlye take heede that that place which naturally goeth before, do also go before in the treatise: And if we should make an Oration of sinne and grace, first wee should speake of sinne before grace; but if the places be utterly seperated, it skilleth not in what order thou do expounde them, unlesse perhappes in confirmation, the one do mynister helpe to the other, for then that is to be expounded in the first place, which being done the other must be holpen.

¶ Of the compound kinde of teachinge.

The Sermon which cōsisteth of the compound kind of teaching, or of compound places, is when certaine compound places, that is to say propositions, and general and particuler sentences are handled, which thing althoughe it be properly done by the Methode of confirmation, and of confutation: yet most commonly it chaunceth that a mixt Methode is added, for if the partes of a proposition be obscure, and darke, resolution shall unfoulde them, and set downe the partes eche part by him selfe. Deuision shal expound the partes set downe. Compositiō afterwardes shall compounde them: and the Methode of confirmation & confutatiō shal proue the compound, and shall confute that which stryueth with it. As if the first petitiō should be propounded to be intreated of halowed

(halowed be thy name) here of necessity, first resolution must be added, which might vnfould this simple propositiō into two parts, into the name of God, & the word halowing. Secōdly deuision would expresse both partes, one after another, with definitions & deuisions. Thirdly composition would compound the parts againe. Now frō hence cōfirmation & confutation mighte be added in their due time. And this precept is alwayes to be folowed, when the parts of a proposition haue neede of an explication, otherwise not at al. Furthermore in parables, resolutiō is to be added ŷ first thou maist put down the parts vnfoulded, & thē apply ŷ same by the cōparison of ŷ thing, to the which the parable doth appertaine, & afterwards frame the lessons and exhortacions, as in the parable which is in ŷ Gospell of the seede: there be fiue partes of that parable. The sower, ŷ seede, the sowinge, the earth, and the fruite. To ŷ sower, God: to the seede, the word: to ŷ sowing, the preacher of ŷ word: to ŷ earth, the hearers of the word: & to the fruit of the seede, the fruite of ŷ word may be cōpared. These beīg once declared thou maist frame lessons & exhortations as the lessons of this present parable are. The first yͤ great care of Almighty God in procuring oure saluation. For heare the Lorde is compared to the diligent husband man. The seconde the dignity of the word. The third, the worthines of the mynisterye. The fourth, that if yͤ word bring not fourth good fruit, it shalbe imputed to vs and the deuil. Furthermore exhortations are to be drawen oute of the end of the parable, for the endes of this presente parable are: That the Lorde mighte styrre vp yͤ hearers to the loue of the word: That he mighte reproue the negligent, and might comforte the obedient. But in this kinde of preachinge there is yet a greater force and wisedome of yͤ Preacher to be requyred. Wherrfore to thende that in this part (which otherwyse is harde enoughe) I maye somewhat ayde and helpe the newe Preachers. I wyl intreate of two thinges in order. First I will shewe the Methode of finding out of places, & then I will declare a waye to handle them eloquently and profitablie, in which two chapters this whole facultye seemeth to consist.

¶ Of the inuention or findinge out of common places.

Lest

LEst any man should take that for a common place which is spoken at all aduentures, euen as they are wont to do, who almost out of euery worde do hunte out some thinge, little regardinge whether the same appertaine to the purpose or no, for that they only seeke this that they may seeme to be greate deuisors and no lesse skilfull craftes men of common places: Rules are necessarye, within the limittes whereof, the minde of the Inquisitour maye be comprehended. And although the matter be greater then that it may be accomplished in few preceptes, yet is it profitable for yonge beginners to keepe certaine common Rules, which they may safely folow to theyr benefite whō they shal instruct. First of al therefore when any text is read, & understanded, the occasion, the briefe summe, & comprehensiō, and the ende, and the use of ẏ texte must be sought out, which thinge, how and in what order it oughte to be done, in the Logitiā his kinde of interpreting before is declared. Secondlye the partes, or the propositiōs of the text must be sought out. And last of al out of these according to the rules following, cōmon places must be drawne, which

which seeme to conduce to the ende of that matter which we haue compounded.

¶ The first Rule.

If the subiecte of the proposition be a singuler bonde, or ende, in steede thereof put by degree and in order his superiours, that is to saye, the forme in the first place. Secondly ỹ kind next. Thirdly if you so thincke good, the superiour and higher kinde. And let these be compounded in order with the predicate of the proposition. Psal. 122 in the begining this is the proposition: I reioyce (sayth Dauid) when it is sayd to mee, let vs goe into the house of the Lord. First make a permutatiõ of the person, after this maner: Dauid reioyseth when it is sayde vnto him, Let vs goe into the house of the Lord. Here according to the rule, first put the name of a kinge. Secondlye of a magistrate. Lastlye of a man. This beinge done, ioyne these in order with the predicate after this maner: It is the dutie of kinges to reioyce in that they haue subiectes which agree with them in Religion: It ought to be a comforte to all men to agree in the worshipping

shipping of God. Behold how many generall sentences, this first and childishe rule doth minister vnto vs, whereof the laste is most common, and may be spread into many particuler arguments: of ẏ certainty wherof we must iudge oute of ẏ rule followinge. The example being confirmed in ẏ subiect, the thing is confirmed in the kinde. Therefore when this facte is approued in Dauid, the thing in the kinde ought not to be disalowed. And on the contrarye syde: the example in the subiect being reproued, in matter is reproued in the kinde. As for example: Ozias the king of Iuda taking an other mãs office vpon him displeased God. Therfore kinges, yea all men which meddle with other mens matters do displease God: for it was ẏ office of the priestes, not of kinges, to offer the insence of a sweete perfewme.

¶ The second Rule.

If in steede of the predicate, superiours bee by degree and in order substituted, as ẏ next formes: & afterwards other, & other kindes, a plẽtiful inuentiõ or finding out of places will ensue thereof. This rule certeinly most oftẽ is to be folowed in other thinges,

thinges, but alwayes in the Historyes of Christe. As for example: Christe healeth ÿ Samaritan Leper calling vpon him. Because this Samaritane is an Ethnicke and a man afflicted. Gather thou from hence ÿ Christe will helpe the afflicted Ethnickes, and all men which cal vppon him. And because out of the particuler actes of Christ, his office generally is gathered, it is lawful to frame a place after this maner. That it is the office of Christ, or of Messias, to helpe the miserable and afflicted callinge vppon him.

¶ The thirde Rule.

If in steede of the subiecte and predicate, thou substitute by order formes & kinds: plenty of common propositions will growe therof. As for example: David committing adulterie was banished ought of his kingdome, Therefore kinges greeuouslye offending and generally all men which liue wickedlye, shall some times or other suffer due punishmente. The filthines of wicked men was drowned in an vniuersall floud, Therfore wicked men at one time or other shalbe punished.

The

¶ The fourth rule to make abstractes.

SOmetimes it is profitable oute of the cõcretes, as the beleeuing woman of a Cananite (Mat.15.) in her necessitye came to Christe, called vppon him, woulde suffer no repulse, but was more earnest, euen as also the ruler of the Synagoge who beleeuing, did also conuert his whole family vnto the Lord. From hence gather thou the proprieties of Fayth, that is to saye, that fayth inforceth a mã, in necessity to come to Christ, to call vppon him for succour, and maketh him earnest to thende he maye obtaine it: & then he proueth the encrease and receyueth it, and at length bringeth forth most acceptable fruictes vnto God. This rule hath his force oute of that place which is called Coniugata, that is to say, things ioyned together. But because those things, which I haue rehearsed concerninge Fayth, are the principall partes of fayth, I haue encluded them in two Verses after this maner.

Vera fides Christũ petit, & rogat, instat, ab ipso,
Impetrat, & crescit, fructificatq; simul.

In En-

In Englishe thus.

True fayth doth seeke for Christ, doth aske
and maketh earnest sute:
Obtaynes of him, and doth encrease
and also bringes forth fruite.

An other example this is. The man is blessed that feareth the Lorde. The common place is. True felicity cõsisteth in the feare of the Lord: the vse of this rule is greate, not onely in inuenting of places, but also in defining of Concretes. For as Aristotle & Rodulphe do teache oute of the discription of Concretes, ỹ definitions of Abstracts are gathered. As for example: if thou wouldest define what godlines is, take first the Concrete in a notable example: As, godly Abraham did feare the Lord, and did worshippe him in true fayth and obedience: Therefore godlines is the feare of the Lord, fayth and obedience towardes him. By this waye Aristotle founde out the differences of many vertues, which they that are studeous in diuinitye, shal easely perceyue, not to be vnprofitable for them.

¶ The fift Rule.

Those thinges are dilligently to be considered which goe before the matter proпounpounded, which are ioyned also wͭ the same, and which of necessitye do followe the same, and are to be included into common places, As Psal 2. Blessed are al they that put their trust in him. First here it followeth oute of the antecedents, ẏ without Christ none are blessed. For if they be then blessed whē they put theyr trust in Christ, without this confidence al men are miserable. This place also, by a contrary sence is cōcluded after this maner: all ẏ put their confidence in Christ are blessed. Therefore all that put not their confidēce in him are not blessed. If they are not blessed, certainly they are myserable. Heare thou seest how this place doth mynister occasiō to reason of the wretchednes of mankind. The second place is of things adioyning, which is framed according to ẏ .4. rule to wit, ẏ true felicity & blessednes consisteth in ẏ cōfidēce which we haue in Christ. The third place that the benefite is vniuersal. For a general proposition is not restrained to any nation or man, but the benefit is offered vnto al which refuse not to put their trust in him. The fourth place, that fayth in Christ is a meane, whereby men are made the partakers of the benefites of Christe.

The

The fift place of the diuinity of Christ, doth follow out of this place: For if fayth is only to be reposed in God, & hee is pronounced blessed that putteth his cōfidence in Christ, it followeth of necessitye that Christe is true God.

¶ The sixt Rule.

The necessary consequence of causes and of effectes, is not to be neglected. For if the cause be set downe, ÿ effecte is supposed to be concluded: as in our Creede, whē we acknowledge God to be omnipotent, Faith from thence draweth forth a double effecte, the one is that God doth bestowe his benefits vppon whom he wil, the other that hee hath power to defend them whom he hath taken into his custodye. But let vs adde a more famous exāple. In the Lords Supper, as oute of a consequence of causes & effects, particuler sentences are to be gathered oute of a true meditation of the Sacrament: Therfore seing that the Lords Supper is a Sacramente of our redemption by the death of Christ. First the celebration of the Supper, doth by little and little put into oure mindes the thoughte of sinne:

For

For the Lorde died for sinne. Secondlye, it admonished vs of the sacrifice accomplyshed for the redemption of mankynde from the lawe of sinne. Thirdly, the dignitie and excellencie of this sacrifice, doth minister vnto godly myndes, the thought, not onely of the greatnes of the wrath of God in striking his sonne for our sinnes, and of the vnspeakeable mercie of God, receyuinge vs vnto his grace, for the sacrifice of his sonne: but also, of the loue of his sonne, making his intercession for vs, and takyng or deryuing his fathers wrath and displeasure vppon hymselfe. Fourthly, contrition springeth out of the thought of synne, and of the wrathe of God. Faythe verely is styrred vp by the vnspeakeable mercie of God, and the loue of his sonne, payinge the pryce of redemption for vs. Fiftlye, this fayth is confirmed and encreased by the vse of the Sacramente so great a thing. Sixtly, faith being confirmed and augmented, doth shewe it selfe acceptable to God, and doth beginne a godlye, honest, and iust lyfe, and loueth his neighbour, with whome hee hath the price of redemption common. Beholde what doctrine and lessons, what plentie, howe godly a meditation of the holy supper, the consequence of causes and effectes doth minister vnto vs an other example. Christe remitteth sinnes of his owne authoritie. Here the effecte doth declare the diuinitie of Christe. The theefe rebuketh his fellowe who was a blasphemer, and calleth vpon Christe, out of which effectes, the contrition, the faith & the newe life of the thefe is to be gathered.

¶ The seuenth Rule.

LEt the repugnauncie of a sayinge, or worde, and the repugnancie of a consequent bee sought out: from whence twoo kyndes of places doe arise. Let the saying be, he that doth teache any other Gospell, is accursed. The repugnancie of this saying is this: hee that teacheth the same Gospell, is not accursed, the consequence of the saying is, that the Pope is accursed, because he teacheth an other Gospell. The repugnancie of this saying is ouerthrowen. As the Pope is not the head of the churche, and we must not obey the Pope.

¶ The eight Rule.

It is

IT is good sometimes by the contrary sense, to frame a place when the termes or boundes be equall, as for example. The iust man liueth by fayth, ergo, hee that is not iuste liueth not by faythe. Whereof it followeth that neither righteousnes nor life, is of woorkes. For so Paule dothe gather it. Gal.3. That no man is iustified by the lawe in the sight of God it is euidēt, because it is written the iust man liueth by faith. In like manner a forme by conterpositiō doth sometimes minister places, as, euery one that is of God doth heare Gods worde. Here the place by conterposition doth gather, that he whiche heareth not Gods woorde, is not of God. These be the principal rules of inuention of places, whose fountaines are places of Logike, & rules of consequences, & there may be more added to them, but I thinke ỹ these are sufficient to newe beginning preachers, which if they wil vouchsafe to folow, they may both haue a ready way to seke out these cōmon places, & also they may iudge well of those places which are obserued by others. Furthermore, hereby they may also iudge what is ỹ cause, why diuers autors do not alwayes shew forth ỹ selfe same places.

The reason of the difference is as well the diuersitie of inuention, as also that other places, do more contente, or please our aucthours. After that the godly preacher hath founde out places, he must enter into a multitude or swarme of places. To this he shall applie a threefolde instrument. For first hee shall diligently consider, whether the place founde out, may expressely, worde for word, be seene in anye place of the Scripture. Secondarely, the place must bee examined by demonstration to an impossible thing, if it be not expressed in the woorde of God. Thirdly, the place must be concluded with some sillogisme, and by a sillogisticall conuersion, it must bee tried as it were with a touchestone. Let this be an example of a demonstration, to an impossible thing. The place to be proued is, that Christians may possesse that whiche is their owne, take the opposite of this place. No Christians may possesse that whiche is their owne. Nowe seke out the proposition whiche is manifestly true, whiche with the opposite sayinge, may be one of the premisses in the sillogisme as for example: all that doe geue Almes, ought to possesse their owne, of which twoo premismisses a moste false conclusion doth follow, to witte, that no Christian man shall giue almes. By the manifest falsenes of this the other of the premisses is to be ouerthrowne, wherfore since ỹ Maior is manifestly true, it followeth that the Minor is false: from hence nowe is inferred the truthe of the place, propounded by the lawe of contradictions. Nowe let vs gather together that whiche we haue sayde. All that should geue almes, ought to possesse their owne. No Christians may possesse their owne: Ergo, no Christian shall geue almes. But the cõclusion is false, ergo, one of the premisses: not the Maior, ergo the Minor, which saith that: No Christians maye possesse their owne. Let this be the example of a sillogisticall conuersion. The place, some hearing Gods worde are not godly. The sillogisme. None that walke after the fleshe are godly, some hearing Gods worde walke after the fleshe: Ergo, some hearing Gods worde are not godly. conuerte it after this manner. If none that walke after the fleshe are godly, and some that here the worde, walke after the fleshe: ergo, some that heare the worde are not godly. For al they that heare the

the worde are not godly. For all they that heare the worde are godly, or els none that walke after the fleshe are godly. None that heare the worde shall walke after the flesh, or els some men that heare the woorde, walke after the fleshe: certaynely some that walke after the fleshe shalbe godlye. but none that do walke after the fleshe are godlye, and some whiche heare the woorde walke after the fleshe. The conclusion therefore remayneth firme and sure, that some whiche heare the woorde are not godlie.

¶ Of the manner of handling of places inuented, both plentifully and profitably.

TO the plentifull and profitable handling of places, foure thynges are chiefly requyred, whereof the firste is, the diductions of questions, that is to saye, of the places inuented. ¶ The seconde a plentiful confirmation. The thirde, the digression to an other matter. ¶ The laste is the artificiall conclusion. I wyll intreate of these foure

foure after that order as they are set downe before your eyes declaryng euerye one of them playnelye with preceptes and examples.

¶ Of the diduction of questions.

HEre wee must speake not of the inuentions of Common places, whereof now we haue intreated, but of ỹ diduction of cōmon places inuented, that is to say, of multiplying them into manye questions or places. Therefore the place inuented is diducted, either into simple places, or into compounde places: as for example. If the fifte commaundement were layde before vs, to be exponnded. First here, thou shalt seeke the common place according to the precept of the firste rule after this manner. Fathers are to be honoured, parentes are superiours, ergo superiours are to be honoured. This common place in the handling of the fifth cōmaundement, is the principall, & chiefly to be touched. But yet ỹ it may plentifully be intreated of, it shalbe expedient to diduct or reduce it into other places, eyther

 simple,

simple, which the very wordes them selues do geue: or compounde, which either do cō-siste of them which are necessarely included in the wordes them selues, as the formes or particular sentences, are included in their kyndes: or generall sentences, and what thinges soeuer are necessarely ioyned with the matter: or els are taken out of them, which are annexed and ioyned to the condicion and state of the matter, as in this example layde before vs, are included two simple places, one of honour, the other of superiours. These are to be handled a sunder, by the simple kinde of teaching of thinges, after the same sorte, as I haue hādled before. Secondly, out of the diuision of this generall sentence: superiours are to bee honoured, many particular sentences do arise, according to the contrary diuision, of the subiecte and predicate. The subiect may be deuided into these formes that of superiours, some are priuate, which are either natural, as parentes: or els not naturall as scholemaisters, patrones, and housholders: some are publike, as the ciuill and ecclesiasticall magistrate, with their differences. Furthermore the predicate (to be honoured) may be deui-

deuided into partes of honour, for he which honoureth an other, doth reuerence him, obey him, and is thankefull vnto him. So there are three partes, or differences of the predicate. From hence as out of a groue, we may gather particular sentences. As we must reuerence our parentes, we must obey our parentes, we must bee thankefull to our parentes, wee must reuerence oure maisters, wee must obey our maisters, wee must bee thankefull to oure maisters, wee must reuerence patrones, wee must obaye patrones, wee must bee thankefull to patrones. After the same manner particular sentences are to bee framed, out of the rest whiche I haue declared, from whence may ensue a moste great plentie of needeful questions. Ouer and besides this, places oftentymes, are profitably taken out of thẽ whiche consist of the state and condition, as: if parentes, scholemaisters, patrones, are frowarde, or ouerthwarte, harde, or cruell, whether then wee should shewe them any reuerence, obedience, or kyndnes? and to what ende? and so out of other conditiõs, questions, are multiplied. But this laste kynde of questions, whiche doth growe out of the

of the cōdition may be handled very fitly by a figure called occupation. Beholde if thou wilt unfolde these particular sentences, by resolution, and wilt handle them by diuisiō, and confirme, and garnishe them with the methode of confirmation: not one sermone, but soe manye as there are particular sentences, may be made, and framed. I confesse that all common places, doe not shewe so great plentie of particular sentences, notwithstanding there is none so barraine, but at the least, it may minister some sentences, which ye may frame out of a cōmō place, by the same reasō which is declared, which thinge that thou maiest doe cunninglye, it woulde muche profite thee if thou haddest skilfull knowledge in the doctrine of predicables, predicamentes, and propositions.

¶ Of a plentious confirmation.

A Plentious confirmation consisteth in the kindes of proofes, in heapinge and in dilating of arguments, and in confutation of the contrary opinion of which we wil speake in order.

¶ Of the kindes of Proofe.

There is a three fould kinde of proofes in Diuinity. The first and most safest kind, is when proofe is brought out of the euidēt and cleare propositions of the Scripture. As for example, Parentes are to be honoured, because the 5. Comaundemēt, euidently and plainly commaundeth: Honour thy father and thy mother. In like case, Righteousnes is of fayth & not of works, because the word of the Lord doth so pronoūce. We hould that a man is iustifyed by fayth wout workes. The second kind is reasoning as oftentimes as it is not pronoūced by plaine woordes, but is gathered by a stronge and vnmouable consequence. And this kinde is double, streight and indirect. The streight is when that which is to bee proued, is gathered plainly in the first conclusion, which kinde is borowed from ẏ place of inuentiō, of the kinde, of the forme, of the definition, of ẏ causes, of ẏ destinates, & of things, adioyning. As if this questiō were asked, whether scholemasters are to be honoured? out of ẏ kinde, or general, thou maiest conclude well that all superiours are to be honored, ergo scholemasters also, but ẏ indirect kind con-

concludeth not simplie, that whiche is set downe to be proued: but doth gather an inconuenience out of the opposite or contrary, wherwith he ouerthroweth the Antecedent which being ouerthrowen the truthe of the opposite immediatly floweth: as if superiours are not to be honoured, neither parẽts are to be honoured, but this is false, ergo, yͤ also. Therefore it followeth superiours are to be honoured. The third kinde is, of lesse reputation, when we laboure in the testimonies, & examples of thẽ, which seme to haue florished in yͤ church, which kinde is disproued, if it be depriued of the former proofes. Let vs propounde an other exãple. And let the question bee whether Christe bee God. This is first proued by a saying, or by yͤ first kind of proofe. For thus is it spokẽ of Christ in the first of Iohn, chap.5. he is true God & life euerlasting. Secondlye by reasoning, Christe hath done the workes pertaining to God of his own proper power, & the honour of God is attributed to Christe, ergo, he is God by the indirect waye: If Christe were only a creature, euery one only were accursed, that would put their confidence in him: but nowe Gods woorde pronounceth them

blessed

blessed which put their trust in him.ergo,he is no creature,but true God. Thirdly, ŷ testimonie of the church,as the crede of Athanasius,and the voyce of all the people,in geuing their consent, do testifie Christe to bee God. Furthermore this our distinction of proofes wãteth neither reason, nor exãple. The reason is this,whatsoeuer is proued,or disproued in sacred thinges,it is needefull ŷ the same be done, either by testimony of the scripture,or of the churche. If it be done by the scripture,it shalbe either by the expresse woordes from whence the firste kinde doth growe,or els intricatly,or obscurely,& that either in ŷ generall,or in the particular sentence,from whence the second kind of proofe is taken. But if any thing be proued by the testimonie of the churche, it shalbe the third kind of proofe. Hereof truly we haue an example of Paule,who in his wryting as it is wel knowẽ,hath vsed this threefolde kinde of proofe. That righteousnes is of faith: by saying or wordes he proueth it when as hee saith:The iust man liueth by faith,by reasoning thus. If righteousnes be of woorkes, Christe died in vayne. From hence now that followeth whiche he propounded,that righteousnes

teousnes is of fayth. By example: Abraham beleeued God, and it was imputed to him for righteousnes. Also wee beleeue in Christe, that wee may be iustifyed by fayth. If these kindes be delated or spoken of at large, there wil aryse great plenty of proofes, but yet a meane is to be kept, lest plenty come out of season, & so breede lothsomnes.

¶ Of the heaping of arguments.

Congeries, or Heape in this place is when in prouing the proposition or cōmon place the Chapters of principal argumentes are added, and as it were gathered together into one bundell, as if this proposition were to be handled. No man is able of his owne strength to fulfil Gods Lawes, the Chapters which followe of the Argumentes, may by heape, be added after this maner: For the experience of all men doth proue this manifestlye. This our wounded nature groning doth acknowledge this, the vniuersall Scripture cryeth oute of this. To conclude the Sacrifyce of the sonne of God, torne after a most horrible maner vppon the gibbet of the Crosse, doth proue vnto vs.

to vs. After this maner, Cicero ioyneth to the proposition, a heape of Arguments, whom in disposinge of Argumentes all the best learned men are wont to immitate and follow. Notwithstanding although Cicero sometimes beginneth frō the last Chapter, a dilatinge of Argumentes put in the Heape, wherunto he ioyneth first, and after goeth forwarde vnto the laste, which is the last in the treatise. Yet for the Deuine and the Preacher, it is the surest way to follow an order in the Heape put in the Exposition.

¶ Of the Exposition or dilating of Argumentes.

Exposition or dilatinge, is by the which an Argument propounded is confirmed and beutifyed. But a copious Exposition consisteth of a proposition, of a reason, of a shewing, the cause of the reason of Exornation, and of Conclusion. The Proposition is that, which setteth before oure eyes some Chapter of an Argument, as though it were the proposition of a confirmation.

The

The reason alloweth the proposition, and it ought to be such a one, as maye be the minor of a sillogisme. AEtiologia, doth shew the cause of the reason, and it is meete, that it be such a one as maye eyther be the maior of a sillogisme, or els the proufe therof: So that a whole sillogisme is made of a proposition, of a reason, and of the cause of the Reason. After the cause of the reason, Exornation shall followe, which is to be borowed of sentences, comparates, contraryes, similitudes, examples. The laste shalbe the conclusion, which gathereth together the summe of the former, and concludeth the principall proposition. These are the preceptes of an expolition, neyther doth that which I haue sayd, striue against the opinion or iudgemente of them which haue nombred seuen parts of an expolicion. For there is not onelye one kinde of expolition, but I haue chosen ÿ onely which I thought to be most meete for preachers, that are but new beginners. But to the ende the preceptes of an expolition may be vnderstanded. I wil put downe one example. I haue before propounded this common place: No man of his owne power or strengthe is able to fulfill

fulfill the lawes of God. Furthermore to this place I haue added foure Chapters of proofe, by a heaping of arguments. Wherof the first was, that the experience of al mē did proue that to be true. Let this Chapter be the proposition of an exposition after this maner. The experience of all men conuinceth this, that no man is able to fulfill the Lawe of God. (the reason) For all men doe easelye perceiue in themselues, howe farre they are from the perfecte and perpetuall obedience of the Lawe of God. (The reason of the cause) For they see that the Lawe of God is holye, and a rule of perfect life: and that they themselues are altogether wicked by nature, and also feeble, and weake (the exornation from ꝑ sentēce.) So that is true whereof the Prophet speaketh, that all oure righteousnes is as the cloth of a menstruous woman: which sentence how cold it consist, if the experience of any wise man had proued the cōtrary. (the exornation from the cōparisons) For euen as a tree whose roote is rotten, and infected with a poysoned sappe cā neuer bring forth but poysoned fruite: so man whose harte is infected with the poyson of sinne, cannot shewe a pure and perfecte obedience to the law of God. (The exornation from the examples) what: did not holye Abell confesse this in his Sacrifice: trulye it is euen so: For God had neuer allowed the Sacrifice of Abell, vnlesse that holy man had knowē Christ to be him which was promised, that should iustifye all beleeuers, & vnderstoode his owne sinne: whereby hee knew himselfe to be hindred, that he coulde not fulfill the lawe of God. For if hee had thoughte himselfe able to fulfill the lawe, he could neuer haue sacrificed a right, that is to saye haue declared in his sacrifice, that the promised seede, shoulde be the fulfiller of the Lawe. Hereunto Dauid also as a moste sufficiente witnes may be added, who crying vnto the Lorde, confesseth openly, that no man is iustifyed in ẏ sight of God. For hee complayneth ẏ all haue erred, and are made vnprofitable, &c. (The conclusion) Since therfore wee haue Dauid as a witnes: since wee acknowledge the poyson of sinne, since we behould the purity of the Law, and our owne vncleannes, who I praye you, (vnlesse hee weare a mad man) woulde denye this: that

hee

hee telleth his owne weake nes, and imbecillitye in rendringe obedience to the Lawe of GOD. In this example after a sorte yee maye see the vse of expolition: whiche if I had determined to haue handled at large, euerye parte beinge dilated and multiplyed, a whole Oration euen oute of the first Chapter of the proofe, woulde plentifullye haue proceeded. After the same order the other three Chapters, which consiste in the heape of Argumentes, must bee handled. From hence studious yonge men maye easelye iudge, that greate profyte commeth of this Expolition. Wherfore they shall take a moste profitable worke in hande, if they will busilye practise themselues in the handlinge of an Expolition. For from hence they shall obtaine suche a facultye and facilitye, that hereafter when they shall haue occasion, eyther to speake of weightye matters, or to preache the worde of GOD, these preceptes of an Expolition shall come into theyr minde, euen as it were vppon a sodaine.

¶ Of the confutation.

The Methode of confutation, which consisteth of proposition, of sublation, of an opposite proposition, and of the solution, is before declared and made manifest by examples: Wherefore in this place I will onely shew the hearers the place of a confutation. The proper place for a confutation is assigned immediatly after the confirmation, which place notwithstanding he hath not alwayes. For so often as any other opinion besydes oure owne dothe occupye the mindes of the hearers, the Exordium or beginninge maye be taken from the confutation: which rule not onely Aristotle and Cicero, but also S. Paule followeth in his Epistle to the Romaynes, for there labouringe to confirme this proposition: that righteousnes is of Faython. First hee confuteth the prejudices or forejudgementes of the Gentiles, and of the Jewes: Of the Gentiles whiche thoughte that they were iustifyed by the lawe of Nature. And of the Jewes who boasted that they were iustifyed by the Lawe giuen unto theym by God.

God. Oute of this confutation of preiudices S Paule falleth into a proposition, which hee firste repeateth, and after ioyneth to it a iust confirmation. My iudgement is that this example of S. Paule is to be folowed, so oftentimes as the hearers mindes are occupied with any other opinions then with their owne.

¶ Of digression.

The preceptes of digression maye be reduced to fiue pointes, which are, Place, meane, matter, time, and the retourne frõ the digression. As cõcerning the place, this is to be obserued that digression oughte to be added vnto anye proposition that is proued. For that is a digression oute of season which is made when the matter is not as yet confirmed. Suche a meane is to bee added, which may not interrupt the memorye of learners, wyth troublesome tediousnes: For they teache vnluckelye, whoe neglectinge the doctrine, and beinge vexed with some small iniurye, doe declaime, and spende whole houres againste some one or other, whom they thincke haue offended them.

theym. The matter of digression appertayneth to exhortations, consolations, chidinges, but not to euerye sorte. For such oughte the matter of Digression to bee, that of his owne accorde, it maye seeme to flowe oute of the Doctrine, and not to bee fetched anye where els. For excepte the force, and nature of Learninge, do offer the matter of digression, it can make nothinge to edification at all. This precepte is therefore more dilligentlye to be obserued, because often tymes they that are vnexercised offende againste it, not withoute great iniurye of the woord of GOD, and hurte of the hearers. In the fourth place I haue put downe Tyme, which of necessitye requireth a Digression, for when the hearers doe eyther abhorre the Doctrine, eyther are somewhat more slouthfull, or els be faint harted, then are they to be chidden, prouoked, and comforted. The retourne from the Digression, oughte not to be violente, but the ende thereof oughte to bee applyed, that it maye bee ioyned with that parte of the Sentence, from whence the Digression was made, whiche canne be scarcelye broughte to passe, vnlesse

lesse the force of the doctrine haue shewed the matter of the Digressiō: or some figure beinge added, it maye haue recourse to the doctrine.

As sone as blessed LVTHER began to defende the doctrine of the Gospell agaynste the tyrannye of the Pope, there was neede of more sharper prickes, and therefore hee was more oftner occupied in Digressions, as maye appeare by his wrytinges. But now (the doctrine is fortifyed and establyshed, and a more peaceable estate restored to oure Churches) wee muste vse these sharper prickes more sparinglye. Furthermore because neyther the vocation is a like, neither the aucthoritye of all men equall, newe Preachers wyll thincke it to be a parte of modestye, seldome to wander beyonde the marke. Notwithstandinge if any shal require examples of the Digression of these preceptes, let him reade the Epistle to the Hebrewes, for that onelye wyll mynister a greate nomber of examples.

¶ Of Artificiall conclusion.

I Haue toulde you before, what manner of conclusion, oughte to be added in the exposition of euerye argumente. In this place wee muste speake of the conclusion of any place or whole Sermon, where in these thinges are to be obserued. First the place explicated, is to be repeated in one proposition. Secondlye a short reconinge of Argumentes is to be ordayned, and especiallye of the chiefeste Chapters. Thirdlye the illation, or inference maye followe in the which three thinges maye bee ioyned which are to be finished in three propositions: what the presente place teacheth, what it confuteth, and what it admonisheth vs of. Fourthlye, al thinges are so to be disposed, that the passage maye be more easye into the place followinge, if manye are to be expounded: as for example, the place which I proponed aboue beinge declared: That no man of his owne power is able to fulfil the Lawe of God, this cōclusion were not vnprofitable (the repetition of the place) whoe nowe after this will thincke himselfe to be able of his owne power to fulfill the lawe of God (the enumeration of argu-

of argumentes) when as not onelye experience and nature do deny it, the scripture in euery corner by manifest testimonies doth confute it: but also the sacrifice of the same doth teache a farre contrary thing (the Illation) wherefore this place teacheth vs all to acknowledge our weakenes and synne, confuteth the Iusticiaries, whiche do boaste of the righteousnes of the lawe, and admonisheth vs all, that confessing our sinnes & weakenes, wee shoulde flie vnto Christe, (the transition) whome the Gospell offereth vnto vs, whereof wee must speake presentlye.

¶ Of that kynde of Sermon which consisteth in exhortation called Parainetical kinde.

The first kinde of preaching being expounded after a sorte (whiche because it consisteth in teaching, I haue named, Διδασκαλικη. Now followeth the other the parenetical kinde whiche therefore I will more briefly handle, for that very seldome it is had alone, and by it selfe, for moste commonly it is wont is wonte to be myngled with the doctrinall kynde. The parenetical kynde is that wherby we perswade or disswade, wee comforte or rebuke the hearers. From hence springeth a threefoulde parenetical Sermone, to witte perswasible, comfortable, and rebukeable, of the whiche these thinges in order are to bee declared. First the difinition, next the inuention, and afterwardes the treatise, to whome I wyll ioyne moste briefe examples, to the intente the preceptes more easelye maye bee vnderstanded.

¶ Of the perswasible Sermon.

The perswasible Sermone is, whereby wee perswade the hearers, either to doe, to suffer, or to forsake some thinge. The places of inuention in this kinde are these especially: the necessitie of the cause, of the commaundement, of the vocation, the priuate and publique commoditie, the dignitie of the persone and the thing. Examples olde, newe, Christian, Ethnicke: Also parables, and sentences, the profes, confirmations, and exornations, of all these maye be sprincled here cled here, and there, and as I haue sayde before in the Logicke Methode, the exhortations, consolations, and rebukes, must be myngled with the figure of digression. So here with the Methode of Confirmation, the pareneticall places oughte to bee confirmed. Moreouer, in this treatyse, fower thynges mete together, the occasion, the proposition, the confirmation, and the conclusion: The occasion reciteth the cause of the exhortation. The proposition must bee amplified, and multiplied, and oftentimes with other wordes, and figures must be iterated. The cōfirmation is to be sought for, out of the places nowe rehearsed, in whiche confirmation moreouer, there are twoo thynges, to be considered, the degree or steere, and the figure. The degree maketh vs by little and little, to ascende from lighter, and lesser matters to weyghtier thynges, and of more importaunce, and so to moste weyghtie and greate matters. Otherwyse exhortation is of no estimation, or pryce. The figure dothe not onelye serue the affections, but also (yf I may so tearme yt, maketh the oration more sharpe and wyttye, to the ende it may altoge-

altogether pearce into the myndes of the hearers, and so possesse the whole harte it selfe. Hereunto interrogation, subiection, exclamation, admiration, dubitation, hypotyposis, dialogisme, Aitopoiija, and others of the like sorte, whiche are named and expounded of Rhethoricians ought to be referred. The conclusion, which I haue made the fourth part of the treatise, hath no neede of newe preceptes, but is to be confirmed by the same meanes, whiche is aboue declared, notwithstanding to the ende that the vse of the preceptes, may be seene, I wil set down one example onely.

The example of the persuasible sermon.

The occasion, because I see many slacke & slowe to heare the worde of God (proposition) I haue determined brieflye to stirre you vp to the loue of the heauenlye woorde, whereby ye are compelled to the more dilligent hearinge and kepinge of the doctrine brought vnto vs from heauen. (the passion of the mynde) although it is to be lamented that mortall men be so vnmindefull of their salua-

saluation, that they haue nede of prickes, to the ende they may make spede thether, whether they ought to be caried with al violēce. (The necessitie of the cause) for therfore such a slothfull heauines is rooted in our mindes because we do not consider, as wee ought to do, what is the necessitie of the heauenlye worde: can any man vnderstande the will of God without his worde? verely if the wisdō of the worlde (as Paule truely affirmeth) is but foolishnes before God, it can not come to passe that wee should knowe the wylll of God, until we haue vnderstoode, the foolishnes of the fleashe. (The necessitie of the commaundement) truely the commaundement of God the father, doth seme to slippe out of our myndes, whose wordes do sounde from heauen: This is my welbeloued sonne heare him. The sonne him selfe doth desire, that his woorde may be heard of them that are his: My sheepe here my voyce: whereof it followeth: that those whiche do contempne the voyce of Christe, whiche he soundeth by his ministers, are not his sheape. The holy ghoste, by the voyce of the Prophetes, and of the Apostles, dothe inuite and call vs to the lawe, and the testimonie. Therfore who

arte

arte thou whiche despisest the commaunde-ment of the eternall father? Who art thou that despisest the sonne whiche suffered for thee, calling thee to the hearing of his word? Who art thou that refusest the dominion & rule of the holy ghost? (the necessitie of the vocation) we are so forgetfull from whence, and wherto we are called: are we not by the worde brought out of the darkenes of Sathan into ẏ marueylous light of God? This worde hath called vs, this worde hath made vs Christians, but wee in the meane season being vnmindefull of so glorious a name, haue contemned the misterie of saluation. (the profit) but and if this royall and noble vocation moueth vs not truely, the reason of our proper cōmoditie ought to moue vs: wherewithall we perceiue that euen ẏ very brute beastes are touched. But who is able by any reason of man or of Aungels, to reci-te at the least but certen porcions of this cō-moditie, specially when Paule after Esaye sayth, the eye of man hath not seene, neither the eare hath hearde, neyther hath it ascen-ded into the harte of man what thynges God hath prepared for them whiche loue hym. Neyther yet is there any cause, why

anye

anye man shoulde dreame that hee loueth God, whiche doth not heare his woorde nor meditate it, neither compareth it to gether, that the misterie which lieth hidde therein, may by little and little be of him the better understanded, for Christe the euerlastinge worde of God, sayth: He that loueth me wil kepe my sayinges, and my father will loue him. To this loue of ẏ father, & of the sonne there are annexed greater good thinges, then whiche by mans capacitie maye bee perceiued. Although Paule hath comprehenced, the summe of them in these wordes: The Gospell is the power of God vnto saluation to all beleuers. O foolishe man, O stony harte, that despyseth, reiecteth and treadeth vnderfoote so great a saluation offered. That wee may prouide for the belly, What do we not? do we not learne artes? do wee not sayle vpon the Seas? wee flye no froste, wee refuse no heate, we slomber at no tyme, to the ende wee maye prouide for our miserable bellye. When these thynges are readye to peryshe, wee are moued, and in the meane season wee leaue our saluation. So great is our madnes, so greate is our peruersnes, & wickednes, we poore misera-

ble wret-

wretches are so muche infected, with the poyson of sathan, that we would with more willing mindes dye in our wickednes, then take holde of the stretched out arme of God and so to be saued. But when wee haue nothing els to do, then wee heare the worde of the Lorde, and that with lesse reuerence truly, thē those three halfpeny seruaūtes which in times past did heare Esope reciting of his fables. Would to God this our negligence were not an euident signe of the punishmēt of our ingratitude. (The dignitie of the persone & of ẏ thing) who would haue thoughe at any time that men are so obliuious, that they should be vnmindefull of their promise made in baptisme, for there they are consecrated to the bodie of Christe, and are made his members, that they may be fellowe cōpaignions with him of heauenlye thinges: neither can we by any other meanes abyde in the body of Christe, then by faythe which commeth by hearing: here, not without a good cause a mā may doubte, whether this may be ascribed to our madnes, or dulnes, that wee oftentymes, moste vngratefullye do reiecte, so greate a dignitie whiche wee haue in the body of Christe, and so greate a treasure

treasure of heauenly goodes, which we possesse by Christ. (examples.) It is maruell that we are not made more wary by other mennes harmes. It is a wonderfull thinge that it sinketh not into our myndes, howe all the worlde perished in the floode, for the contempte of Gods woorde. Wee are not moued by the examples of the holye patriarches, Abell, Seth, Enoch, Noe, Abraham, and of a greate sorte, who nowe enioye the moste ioyfull presence of God in heauen. I reioyce sayth Dauid when it is sayde to mee, let vs goe into the house of the Lorde. But we on the contrarie side reioyce, whē the worlde dothe inuite vs to pleasures, wherewith not withstandyng wee are bayted tyll at the lengthe we hange, snared and taken vppon the hooke. Blessed is hee sayth the same Dauid, whiche dothe meditate in the Lawe of God daye and nyghte. But wee (O griefe to tell) do not otherwyse flye from the meditation of the heauenly worde, then if all these thinges which are set before vs in the worde were but fearfull thynges to feare chyldren withall. The Tomuri priestes of Dodonæ, neuer departed out of the temple whiche notwithstanding did embrace deuelishe superstition, in stede of the worde of God: wee neuer, or seldome, do enter into the churches, who are not withstanding enstructed by the worde, & by manifoulde testimonies, in our religion, but woulde to God wee weare instructed, woulde to God wee woulde thynke, that in our hartes, whiche wee professe with oure mouthe and tongue: whiche if wee woulde do, wee would not so obstinatly cōtemne the ministrie of the worde. What aunswere I praye thee, wilt thou make to the sonne of God, when he in ẏ last day shal shew to thee his woundes? when hee shall accuse and condemne thee, for his bloude cruellye troden vnder thy foote, then shall that verelye happen vnto thee, whiche the Lorde hath fore spoken shall comme to passe: that for shame and the iust iudgement of God, with the wicked companie of the damned, thou shalt say to the mountaynes fall vpon vs, & that for this cause, leaste thou shouldest beholde the face of the sonne of God, whome here thou haste despysed, whose worde thou haste here reiected, whose bloude thou hast cruelly trodden vnder foote, whome stretching out his armes, wette and bespotted with

with bloude, and desyrous to delyuer thee out of the myddle of death, and the Jawes of Hell, thou wretche haste despysed: A wretche in deede, and suche a one, as the iust iudge, (vnlesse thou repent) wyll cast into euerlasting darkenesse, and pryson. (The conclusion.) Let vs praye vnto God therefore, that hee woulde converte vs, by whom beinge conuerted, wee mighte bee moued with the sweetenes of the worde of God, that hee woulde styrre vs vp with his spirite, to heare the worde of saluation, by the whiche wee maye learne, the wyll and true worshipping of God, by the whiche so many cõmodities, come to vs, by ỹ which so many Patriarches, Prophetes, Apostles, Sainctes, Martyres, and manye other godlye men, haue obtayned saluation, by the which the righte waye is shewed to vs, by Jesus Christe our Lord: to whom with the father and the holy ghoste, be prayse honour & glory, worlde without ende. Amen.

This example of a treatise, after a sorte, doth shewe the vse of the places of inuention: I haue myngled a fewe figures, I haue somewhat more often touched the proposition, neyther am I ignoraunte, that this my treatise of example, is farre inferiour vnto the dignitie of the matter. Wherefore, I councell them that are studious that whyle they maye, they often exercise them selues, in declayming in wryting that hereafter they may come the more furnished to the function, of the moste sacred ministerie, the whiche to defile with longe pattering, and vnlearned bablinge, is a thing moste wicked.

¶ Of the consolatorie Sermone or whiche consisteth in comforting.

The Consolatorie or comfortable sermon is, wherein the preacher, doth lift vp the man afflicted, and striuing vnder the crosse, leaste being ouercome with impatience, he should be subdued, and ouercomme with sorowe. These are especiallye the commune comfortable places. The firste is the wyll of the heauenly father. The seconde, the condicion. The thirde, the promise of deliueraunce. The fourth, the nececessitie of the conformitie of Christe, and his mẽbers. The fifth, the commoditie whiche is manifould.

fould. For by the crosse the presumption of a mans owne power, is ouerthrowen, hipocrisie is disclosed, confidence in the fleshe is shaken of, obedience is confirmed, pacience is proued, contempte of the worlde followeth, humilitie ensueth, erroure paste is corrected, euill to come is taken hede of before hande, faythe is exercised, hope is taughte to be reposed in oure God. Reade more concerning this matter in the places of Philip Melancthon. The treatise consisteth of occasion, proposition, confirmation, and conclusion, euen as in the perswasible kynde, to whiche it is lyke, moreouer because it is profitable to knowe a certayne waye of applying of comfortes, I wyll brifly declare the Methode of comforting.

The Methode of geuinge of comforte.

BUt leaste consolation shoulde be applyed out of season, or unskylfully, wee wyll distinguishe. Firste, betweene pryuate, and publique comfortes, and afterwarde describe the iuste forme of them both. I call that a priuate consolation, whiche happeneth to one

one alone oppressed with some griefe or crosse. I call that commune whiche in the tyme, either of persecution or of any plague sent from God, falleth vpon the whole congregation: But firste, wee wyll entreate of the priuate, in whiche threateninges are generallye to bee obserued. Firste, who it is that is to be lifted vp with consolations. Secondlye, what it is that doth grieue him. Thyrdlye, a fitte application of the medicine to the present griefe. Hee that feeleth payne or griefe, eyther is godlye or vngodlye: If hee bee godlye, streightwaye the cōmon inheritaunce of the sonnes of God being shewed, hee is to be lifted vp, to be comforted, and cherished with consolations, and that by the places aboue rehersed, and here with muche profite the eight chapter to the Romaines, may be alledged. But if hee be vngodly, it is nedefull as in a greeuous disease, that a greater care bee applyed, for suche a one is not to bee lyfted vp streyghtwaye, but is so muche the more to bee caste downe, with the thundryng of the Lawe of God, and to bee beate downe with threateninges, vntyll hee acknoweledge his owne vngodlynes without hipocrisie, vntyll hee

vnder-

vnderstande the wrath of God to bee styrred vp agaynst hym, vntyll hee crye wyth Manasses, that hee is gyltie manye wayes. For hee that applyeth comforte by and by, to a wycked man, eyther sycke, or otherwyse oppressed with anye calamitie dothe applye a moste daungerous an vnseasonable, and a deadlye poyson. And doth much lyke to that Phisicion whiche healeth the wounde outwardlye, the matter of putrifaction remaynyng within, from whence afterwarde a greater wicked and deadly mischief bursteth out. Wherfore as the skilfull Phisition, the tent being put in often, draweth out the corrupt matter, whiche beynge drawen foorth, couereth the wounde ouer with a mollifying playster: So the godlye preacher, should firste touche the byle of the wycked man, by the threatening of the law, that his disease beynge knowen, maye the more easelye bee cured, for it is truelye sayde, that the firste steppe to healthe, is to knowe the disease. The seconde thynge, which in consolations I haue sayde, should be considered, is the thyng whiche causeth the grief, or ẏ thing which doth greue him, whiche I thinke needefull to bee examined, for the righte application of the medicine, for hee is otherwyse to be lifted vp, whiche by his owne faulte hath brought a mischiefe vpon hym selfe. And he also otherwyse to whome by an other mans faulte, euill happeneth. For if any man by his owne faulte hath brought a crosse vpon him selfe, as infamie, pouertie, sickenes, death, &c. The medicine or comforte is not to bee applied forthwith vnles thou see the guiltie person earnestlye touched with the feeling of his synnes, for then this feeling of synnes, is to be confirmed with the worde of God, and to be augmented, if neede shall require. Then wee muste descende to consolations: but if hee bee either an hipocrite, or otherwyse wycked, so longe the curse of the Lawe, and the wrath of God are to bee set before his eyes, vntyll hee knowe the greuousnes of his synnes, and confesse the same to hym selfe oute of the gryefe of hys mynde. But if hee can not bee broughte thereunto by the Lawe of God, and threatenynges, a precious stone is not to bee caste before Swyne. On the contrary parte: If the guyltie persone, shall bee broughte to the knowledge of hym selfe, and bee touched with

with the true feeling of griefe, for his sinne committed: then at length the arte of Phisicke is to be applyed, and these three in order are to be expounded. First his fall, next the punishment, and lastly the ende of both. The fall is to be taughte first to proceede of this, in that he did caste from him the feare of the Lorde: and that may be confirmed fitlye and plentifully out of the first Chapter of S. Paule to the Romaynes. Secondlye that nowe the deceites of the deuill, the filthines of the fleshe, and the wantonnes of the worlde, mighte more easelye preuaile against him, being as it were vnarmed. The fall beinge declared, and confirmed wyth these causes. In the seconde place, wee must declare, that the punishment, is in no wise equal with the offence committed, but is a testimonye of two most contrarye thinges that is to saye of the wrathe of GOD and also of his fatherlye good will and clemencye: of the wrathe of God, if the guiltye person will not repente, and not suffer himselfe to be corrected, with the scourge of God: Of his fatherlye good will and clemencye, if hee being corrected, be made better by the punishmente, and will flye to the

hauen

hauen of repentaunce. After this in the thirde place, the ende both of the fall, and also of the punishment, is to be declared. Of the fall to thend afterward he may be more circumspecte and warier. Of the punishmente in that by the singuler councell and purpose of God (when in the meane tyme hee spareth manye wicked and mischeuous men) hee is chastened, not to the ende hee should perishe, but that he may haue a ready testimonye of his fatherly good will towardes him. But because this will verye hardly perswade him that laboureth vnder the Crosse, witnesses and examples are to be broughte forth oute of Gods worde, such testimonies verelie as these are: Paule the 1. Epistle to the Corinthiās ỹ 11. Chapter saith, that we are chastened with aduersity of the Lord: least we should be damned with the world. See, the end of the Crosse is, least we should be damned, if to witte being admonished by the Crosse we repent againe. My sonne (sayth Salomon) do not
Pro. 16. refuse the correction of the Lord, neither be thou weary whē thou art reproued of him, for whom God loueth hee chasteneth, & yet embraceth him as ỹ father doth his sonne.

The

The aucthour of ye Epistle to the Hebrues the 12. Chapter sayth that we are bastards and not sonnes, if wee be without discipline and correction, suche like places are moste fitte, wherewith the minde of the guiltye person now beinge penitent, maye be lifted vp, that nowe he woulde suffer any kinde of punishmente as one readye to obeye God: let the examples be Manasses, Dauid, the sister of Moses, Kinge Vsias, the people ledde into Captiuitye, and manye others, whiche were punished for certaine sinnes, and after throughe repentaunce, haue retourned home againe. The example of the theefe in comparison of others is famous, who hath set foorth a notable example of patience and fayth. Hee did not therfore compte himselfe an abiecte because hee suffered soe shamefull a death for his wickednesse, but pacientlye sustayned the deserued punishmente, by Faythe reposed in CHRISTE. After suche like testimonies & examples, wherwith the iudgemẽts of God are to be made knowne, in cõparing the manners of men in oure age, with the maners of the people in the olde time: For God is alwayes like to himselfe: (whether thou

thou hast respect to punishment or mercy) the common places before mencioned maye be added. But if that which greeueth him doe come through an others mans faulte, that order in applyinge of comforte is to be folowed, which in a common comfort I am aboute to declare, whereto we must speake at this time. That common comfort therefore maye be rightlye framed, three thinges are to be obserued. First from whence cōmon calamitie procedeth. Secondly which be causes thereof. Thirdly the applyinge of the Comforte according to the difference of the calamity and of the causes. The calamity is eyther sent frō God, or els brought in by the ennemyes of our Common weale. If the calamitye be of God, as the plague, wante of foode and vittaile, droughte and tempestes, the causes are not to be soughte for without vs, but in our owne houses, and within our selues, for the sinnes of perticuler men are the causes of common calamities, and oftentimes for one mans fault the whole common wealth is plagued: whereof Achā, Dauid, OEdipus, and manye others are witnesses, who by their owne wickednes haue brought in a common calamitye.

tye. Here it is no harde matter to applye a comfort, if wee will followe the examples of the holy Prophetes: for the examples of them do teache vs, what is to be done: for they are wont openly to rebuke wickednes, and that after three sortes or kindes of wickednes, to witte: The forsaking of God, hypocrisye, iniurye done to the neighboure and such like, as most chiefelye seeme to abounde amonge the people. Examples are extant heare and there in the wrytinges of the Prophetes. Againe they are wonte to call publickly together al the congregation to repentaunce, fastinge and prayer. Certaine notable examples of these two thinges are of late yeares set forthe, at the commaundement of our most noble King, by the mynisters of oure Churches, not withoute greate profite and mittigation, of deserued punishmentes. Last of al the Prophetes were wont to admonishe them, whō they perceyued to bee defiled with wickednes, more then others, leauing an example to oure mynisters of the worde, that they should admonishe, rebuke and correct them priuatelye) whom they perceiue, by theyr idolatry, vsurie, adulterye, tirannye, deceites,

tes, couetousnes &c. to bring in a plague to ỹ whole cõmon wealth. Tyresias, although he were an Ethenicke priest did call Oedipus the tyraunte, (for whose mischeuous deede, the Theban cõmon wealth was punished with the pestilence,) to painefull penaunce. And after this maner Esaye and Ieremye haue corrected and reprehended the kinges of their time, and haue ascribed common calamities vnto theym. And the ministers of the word ought to knowe that this is not the least part of their function & duty, which if they neglect eyther for feare or sluggishnes, they shall suffer greeuous punishments of God, as in the threatnings of Ezechiell is declared, and els where. But if either priuate or publicke calamitye doe come from men, it is either for Iustice or not. If for Iustice, wee muste then take the comforte from the common condition of the sonnes of God in this worlde, & declare of how great honour God reputeth vs worthie, ỹ hee hath marked vs with a peculier proper marke of his warfare and exercise. Wherefore the Apostles being scourged do reioyce for that they are counted worthye to suffer reproche for the name of Christe: for

For this kinde of crosse is most proper vnto the faithfull, wherewith Christe wilbe glorifyed in vs, euen as S. Peter teacheth in the fourth Chapter of his first Epistle. But if not for Iustice the common calamity be brought vs from men, then the causes are to be soughte oute in our selues, and as before I haue said wheras I haue spoken of the Crosse or affliction sent from God: the comforte is to be applied. Out of these I thincke it is manifest by what waye & meanes both priuate and publicke comforts are to be applyed.

¶ Of the chidinge Sermon.

The Chidinge Sermon is that in the which the preacher chydeth eyther the loytring or the offendinge, or the stubburne and disobediente hearer. The ende of this oughte to be the correction and the amendment of him which is rebuked. Here these places are chiefely to be considered. The first, the filthines of the thinge committed. The seconde, thinges adioyninge or appertayning: as are an euill conscience, the peril of reiec-

of reiection, or to be a caste awaye, and the feare of God, his iudgement hanging ouer our head, and of the present and euerlasting paynes. The third a conference together of the dignity of the person and of the filthines of the thing. The fourth, examples. The fifthe the knitting or ioyning together of the person, as Christe our head and king, the Church which is the spiritual country, our body which is dedicated to God, that it may be ÿ tẽple of God, hereunto the cõmon weale the house the familye &c. maye be referred. When I recken these places, I doe not thincke that all are to be applyed in euery chiding, but now these, sometimes the other, euen as the wise Preacher shall see to be expedient. Let the example be taken out of the first Epistle to the Corinthians & the 6. Chapter, where S. Paule rebuketh fornicatours. The Methode of a treatise is not unlike to the treatise of an exhortation. Wherfore I thincke it not needeful to adde any example: especially, whẽ the places are so plaine, and it is knowen that all thinges are to be proued, allowed, and garnished by the Methode of confirmation. But here I thoughte it needefull to adde twõ thinges.

The

The first that the minde of him which is to be chidden, must bee mollifyed to beare chidinges paciently, which thing may very fitlye be done, if the mynister declare his dutye towardes the giltye person, and shewe the common necessity layed vpon him to do the same, least the chiding shoulde seeme to proceede of some noughtye affection: So S. Paule did before hand mollify the mindes of the Corinthians, before hee vsed sower and bitter chidings. The second that conditions of repentaunce may be mingled, least any being discouraged, with somwhat more rougher chidinges, shoulde fall into desperation or wilfullye kill himselfe.

These are the things good audience which I haue thoughte needefull to be declared, to newe Preachers, and I truste (vnlesse my opinion do foulye beguile mee) that yonge men shal not be a little holpen by declaring this Methode. For all the preceptes which are recited by mee are taken oute of the fountaines of Logitians and Rethoriciās, and are applied to the vse of the Preacher profitable both to the exposition of the holy writers, and also to the makinge of sacred Sermons, wyth the which if yonge men will suffer themselues to be ruled, I doubte not to promise them an easier proceeding in deuine studies, and makinge of Sermons. But because it is not sufficiente to haue inuented fitly, or to haue ordered and disposed those things which we are about to speake of wiselye, vnlesse blessed Memorie be also present. I will adde a few thinges of Memerie in steede of a conclusion to this Methode: and that not after the maner of the olde fathers whoe did inuente Images and signes, which were as certaine notes and helpes of Memorie, (for this subtiltye of witte, I willinglye leaue to theym) but I will gather those thinges onelye, wherewith they ẏ are desirous to learne to make Sermons, shall perceiue themselues to be much holpen.

¶Of Memorie.

LEt vs appointe two maner of wayes of helpinge the memorie, whereof the former is more artificiall, ẏ latter more rude, and rusticall: that which is more artificiall doth consist of two thinges, that is to witte, of order and nomber, for by these it is manifest

fest that artes are both taught and learned. For as order placeth euerye thinge in his proper place, & considereth the beginnings, proceedinges, and markes or ends: so doth nomber measure thinges together, & their partes and porcions. Because therefore the Methode which I haue taught, doth shewe an order of things and as it were nombreth the partes, the best way of learning by hart is diligently to consider the same order in ÿ minde, for it cannot bee, that he which hath conningly framed an order of thinges, and hath obserued the least pointes of thinges & as it were nombered them, but that he may easelye kepe the same in minde, and require the same againe of it, when and as often as he shall haue occasion to speake: whereby it maye seeme a foolishe thinge to prescribe any other way of learning by hart, especiall to those men which are taughte and exercised in the art of eloquent speakinge. Notwithstanding although these thinges in very deede be thus, yet are they not forthwith perceiued of all men. Wherefore that these may be vnderstode more orderly, and maye be applied more nearer to the vse of ÿ preacher, I will deuide this whole reason of learning

learning by hart which I haue said, to consiste of order and nomber, into foure members or preceptes. The first is that he understand the matter perfectly, and minding to preach, do kepe in minde a certaine briefe comprehension of the whole matter. The second member is, that he haue the places, that is to saye κεφάλαια as the Greekes do terme it) by nomber. The third member is, that he make deuisions of the places, that are to be handled, which is needefull to be comprehended in a certaine nomber, which if it may be done by any Uerse, fit for the same, it shall not be unprofitable: as if the use of the lawe weare to be expounded. First hee mighte not unfitly make a thirde deuision, which hee mighte comprehende in this Uerse.

Iustruit, & damnat sontes, docet atque renatos.

In English thus.

It doth instruct, and eke condemne,
all such as godly are:
And to enforme the newe borne men,
it hath as equall care.

And because the first part of this diuisiō,

hath

hath many parcelles, and causes, he might, comprehende them also in this verse:

Mandatum, pœnæ, pax publica, dux ad Iesum.

The paynes and the commaundement, and also publike peace:
The guide and leader vnto Christe.

The trewe meditation of the Law (Doctor Peter Palladius, oure moste watchfull Bishop, very muche deseruing of the churches of the Danes, of Noruegia, and Iselandia) hath comprehended in this verse:

Lex quid eram, quid sum, quid ero, per quem manifestat.

In Englishe thus:

The Lawe doth make apparant what I was, and what I am:
What I shalbe it doth declare,
and eke by whome it came.

The fourth mẽber is, that in certaine places digressions into threateninges, consolations, and exhortations be placed, leaste in making digression to an other matter, the memory be hindered, and the preacher withdrawen from the matter proposided, which commõly is wonte to happen, to thẽ which do not obserue this precept. Nowe when as according to these fower preceptes, hee that will

will preache hath disposed his Oration, and as it were reconed it. Hee must settle him selfe to learne it accordinge to the order of his disposition. And firste of all, hee must commit to memorie the briefe, and summarie comprehension, for that is first to be recited. Secondly, he must learne the places, or the chapters a sonder. And thirdlye the treatise or handlindling of the places with their diuisions and the parcels of them. I doubte not but this waye of learninge by harte, is the best of all, whiche all learned men without doubt do followe. Furthermore, the latter reason whiche I sayde is more rude and rustical, is profitable to men vnlearned, which haue not tasted of the arte of Rhethoricke. And this whether it be framed with notes of nũbers, or with letters, it is all one, and it may be done in this mãner. First, those thinges whiche a preacher ignoraunt of artes will learne by harte, hee shall deuide with notes of number, or with euery letter. Afterwarde in repeting, hee shall see what he hath sette downe at euery note or letter. Last of all, he shall learne by harte according to the distinctions whiche he hath made, and shall demaunde agayne of euery of euery note or letter, as a thing commicted to their custody that whiche before hee had cōmitted vnto them. It will not a litle profite him if firste hee wryte out his Sermone, and afterwarde according to the prescript rules do diuide, and learne it by harte. For the minde doth more easelye retayne and kepe that whiche the hande before hathe noted.

FINIS.

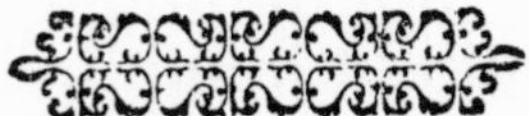